1006802076

MILESTONES
IN MODERN
WORLD HISTORY

The Chinese
Cultural Revolution

MILESTONES
IN MODERN
WORLD HISTORY

1600 · · · 1750 · · · ·

1940 · · · 2000

The Bolshevik Revolution

The Chinese Cultural
Revolution

The Collapse of
the Soviet Union

D-Day and the Liberation
of France

The End of Apartheid
in South Africa

The Iranian Revolution

The Treaty of Versailles

The Universal Declaration
of Human Rights

MILESTONES
IN MODERN
WORLD HISTORY

600 · · · 1750 · ·   · · · 1940 · · · 2000

The Chinese
Cultural Revolution

LOUISE CHIPLEY SLAVICEK

CHELSEA HOUSE
PUBLISHERS
An imprint of Infobase Publishing

The Chinese Cultural Revolution

Copyright © 2010 by Infobase Publishing

Chelsea House
An imprint of Infobase Publishing
132 West 31st Street
New York, NY 10001

Library of Congress Cataloging-in-Publication Data

Slavicek, Louise Chipley, 1956–
The Chinese Cultural Revolution / Louise Chipley Slavicek.
  p. cm. — (Milestones in modern world history)
Includes bibliographical references and index.
ISBN 978-1-60413-278-6 (hardcover)
1. China—History—Cultural Revolution, 1966–1976—Juvenile literature. 2. China—Politics and government—1949–1976—Juvenile literature. I. Title.

DS778.7.S682 2009
951.05'6—dc22   2008054885

Text design by Erik Lindstrom
Cover design by Alicia Post
Composition by Keith Trego
Cover printed by Bang Printing, Brainerd, MN
Book printed and bound by Bang Printing, Brainerd, MN
Date printed: December 2010
Printed in the United States of America

10 9 8 7 6 5 4 3

This book is printed on acid-free paper.

CONTENTS

"A Revolution Is Not a Dinner Party"

"A revolution is not a dinner party, or writing an essay, or painting a picture, or doing embroidery; it cannot be so refined, so leisurely and gentle, so temperate, kind, courteous, restrained, and magnanimous."[1] Mao Zedong, China's supreme leader for nearly three decades following the founding of the Communist People's Republic of China (PRC) in 1949, first spoke these words as a young activist trying to incite his country's downtrodden masses to rebel in 1927. Forty years later, Mao's famous saying would be widely used to justify the shocking brutality and destructiveness of his campaign to stir up rebellion among the Chinese masses: the Cultural Revolution.

MURDER AND MAYHEM

Generally considered as one of history's most horrific political and social upheavals, the Chinese Cultural Revolution lasted from 1966, when Mao and the Chinese Communist Party (CCP) he headed formally launched the radical movement, until the autocratic leader's death a decade later. The Cultural Revolution's central aims were to revitalize the revolutionary fervor of the Chinese people and to speed up the PRC's evolution into a Communist utopia, in which all property was equally shared. To achieve these goals, all cultural remnants of China's capitalist and feudal past were to be ruthlessly destroyed, along with all "persons in authority"—from schoolteachers to top party officials—who were not totally committed to Mao's radical principles.[2]

Mao turned to China's young people to act as the advance guard for his new Cultural Revolution. Taught from earliest childhood to idolize Mao as not only the Communist state's chief founder but also as the source of all wisdom, millions of secondary school and college students enthusiastically answered the call of their "great teacher" and "supreme commander."[3] On school campuses across the nation, the students organized themselves into paramilitary "Red Guard" units, which publicly humiliated, tortured, and murdered teachers, local party officials, and others whom they judged were insufficiently devoted to their commander and his revolutionary ideals. Egged on by Mao, Red Guards also launched a ferocious crusade against China's rich cultural heritage, burning or smashing ancient temples, artwork, books, and other relics of the nation's feudal past.

From the start, violence was a central feature of the Cultural Revolution. In 1967, however, the revolution's death toll escalated sharply as Red Guards and other mass radical organizations splintered into rival factions and began fighting one another in massive street battles. Bloody armed clashes involving thousands of members of contending radical groups

"Bursting with Joy"—a propaganda poster created during the Chinese Cultural Revolution, circa 1970. Although this illustration depicts citizens happily embracing the revolution, the period is today considered one of the most destructive in Chinese history.

erupted in Shanghai and other major Chinese cities, forcing factories, government offices, and schools to shut down and severely disrupting the nation's economy. With the PRC seemingly on the brink of civil war, even Mao had to admit that his Cultural Revolution had gone too far. In 1968, the CCP chairman reluctantly called on the army to rein in the radicals and restore order in the nation's cities. Soon after, he began exiling his revolutionary shock troops, the Red Guards, to remote rural villages to labor in the fields with the peasants.

"MAO ZEDONG THOUGHT" AND THE PEOPLE'S LIBERATION ARMY

Aphorisms—short sayings embodying a general truth—have long been an essential component of Chinese folk literature. After Lin Biao ordered Chinese soldiers to study Mao's writings in the early 1960s, a number of aphorisms lauding the superiority of "Mao Zedong Thought" began to circulate among the People's Liberation Army rank and file. The following is a selection of some of the most popular of the sayings:

All rivers in the world flow to the sea,
All truths are found in the works of Mao Zedong. . . .

Each word in Chairman Mao's works
Is a battle-drum,
Each sentence is the truth.

Dearer than rain or dew to the parched crops
Are Chairman Mao's works to our troops. . . .
If you don't study Chairman Mao
You will be blind;
If you do
A red sun will light your mind. . . .

Heads may fall
Blood may flow;
But never let go
Of the thought of Mao Zedong.*

---

* Quoted in Michael Schoenhals, ed., *China's Cultural Revolution*, pp. 188–190.

The scattering of the Red Guards into the hinterlands had brought an end to the Cultural Revolution's mass-driven violence in most of China by 1969. Savage, state-sponsored persecution of suspected anti-Maoists and "counterrevolutionaries" continued well into the 1970s, however. The most prominent target of the government-led terror campaign was the PRC's second-most powerful political leader, CCP vice chairman Liu Shaoqi. Liu's efforts to strengthen China's faltering economy through moderate, market-oriented reforms during the years leading up to the Cultural Revolution had infuriated Mao, who viewed Liu's policies as a rejection of both his own authority as CCP chairman and of his Communist ideals. In retaliation, Mao had Liu removed from all of his political offices early in the Cultural Revolution, and in late 1968, Liu was formally charged with being a rightist traitor and was imprisoned. After being repeatedly denied medical treatment, Liu died from pneumonia in a squalid makeshift jail a little more than a year later.

IN THE WAKE OF THE CULTURAL REVOLUTION

By the time the Cultural Revolution ended following Mao Zedong's death in September 1976, the brutal political movement had cost the lives of an estimated 3 to 4 million Chinese men, women, and children and had physically or psychologically scarred untold millions more. In the wake of the devastating upheaval, Deng Xiaoping, a moderate who had been purged from the government on Mao's orders during the Cultural Revolution, was able to push aside the chairman's handpicked successor to claim leadership of the CCP and the nation.

To undo the grave harm done to China's economy between 1966 and 1976, Deng instituted a series of liberal economic reforms that would have dismayed Mao, including such blatantly capitalist policies as encouraging private business ventures. Thanks to Deng's decidedly un-Maoist reform program, a few years after the Cultural Revolution ended, China was well on its way to becoming the economic powerhouse it is today. Mao had hoped the Cultural Revolution would help to preserve his radical legacy long after he was gone by cleansing the CCP, and Chinese society in general, of all capitalist practices and influences. Ironically, the cruel excesses and senseless waste of Mao's decade-long movement ensured the exact opposite.

The Rise of
Mao Zedong

From the creation of the People's Republic of China (PRC) in 1949 until his death at the age of 82 in 1976, Mao Zedong was the key figure behind virtually every major political, economic, and social policy adopted by the Communist state. Mao's meteoric rise from modest beginnings in a remote Chinese farming village to absolute ruler of the world's most populous country owed a great deal to not only his political and military skills, but also to his driving ambition and utter ruthlessness.

GROWING UP IN SHAOSHAN

Mao Zedong was born on December 26, 1893, in the small rural village of Shaoshan in China's Hunan province. He came into the world during a difficult and unsettled period in Chinese

history, when Western governments and traders bent on exploiting China's rich natural and economic resources were challeng-
ing the nation's independence. During the half century before
Mao's birth, the members of the Qing Dynasty, China's ruling
family, were intimidated by the modernized armies and techno-
logical expertise of foreigners, and so they repeatedly caved in
to the outsiders' demands for economic and political "spheres of
influence" in their vast yet backward kingdom. By the end of the
nineteenth century, all the major European nations and Japan,
Asia's leading military and industrial power, had wrested a host
of humiliating concessions from the Qing government, including railway, mining, naval, and trading rights in strategic areas
throughout the Chinese Empire.

In sharp contrast to its highly industrialized and urban-
ized exploiters, China was overwhelmingly rural and agrar-
ian during Mao's youth. As had been true for innumerable
centuries, the vast majority of Chinese were landless, illiterate
peasants. Forced to rent their farm fields at high rates from a
tiny group of well-off landlords, most lived in abject poverty.
Mao Zedong's family in the farming community of Shaoshan
was the exception to the rule. They were middling peasants,
as the relatively small number of Chinese farmers who tilled
their own plots of land generally was known. Using money he
had painstakingly saved from his wages during a stint with the
army as a young man, Mao's father, Rensheng, had purchased
2 acres (0.8 hectares) of rice paddy in Shaoshan. A shrewd
businessman, he soon was supplementing his farm income by
buying rice from his poorer neighbors and then reselling the
grain at a marked-up price to merchants in a nearby port town.
With the profits from his farming and commercial ventures,
Rensheng built a spacious, tile-roofed house for his growing
family. Although he and his wife eventually would have four
children, Rensheng's house was so large that Mao always had
his own bedroom, "an almost unheard-of luxury" in Shaoshan,
according to author Philip Short.[1]

A 1910 photograph of the young Mao Zedong with his father, Mao Rensheng. When Rensheng reluctantly agreed to pay for his son's studies, Mao left the life of a peasant behind him.

Reasoning that his eldest son would be more useful to the family business if he could read, write, and do arithmetic, Rensheng enrolled Mao in the village school when he was eight. There, Mao would study with the sons of other middling farmers, the only residents of Shaoshan—aside from the landlords—who could afford the yearly tuition. Five years later, when Mao turned 13, Rensheng decided Mao had had enough schooling. Mao was to work full-time on the farm, Rensheng informed his son, laboring in the rice paddies during the day and balancing the family accounts at night.

Traditionally, Chinese children were expected to obey their parents in all things. Nonetheless, Mao nagged his father relentlessly to let him continue his education. Headstrong and ambitious, Mao had little intention of spending the rest of his life as a rice farmer in little Shaoshan. Two years after being pulled out of the village school, Mao talked his father into sending him to an expensive higher primary school just outside Shaoshan. Mao devoted himself to his studies, and in early 1911 won admission to a respected secondary school in the capital of Hunan province, Changsha. That spring, after Rensheng reluctantly agreed to pay the school's hefty tuition fees, Mao happily left Shaoshan for the bustling capital city. "At seventeen," historians Jung Chang and Jon Halliday write, Mao "said goodbye to the life of a peasant."[2]

FINDING A "ROAD"

By the time he started secondary school in Changsha, Mao had developed a deep interest in the plight of his exploited homeland. Like many Chinese, he had come to believe that the first steps in driving out the hated foreigners and building a stronger China were to rid the nation of its ineffectual imperial rulers and transform the backward-looking empire into a modern, Western-style republic. In October 1911, just six months after Mao arrived in Changsha, supporters of a popular republican reform movement spearheaded by Dr. Sun Yat-sen launched a full-scale revolt against the tottering Qing regime. When the uprising spread to Hunan, Mao dropped out of school and enlisted in the new republican army. By January 1912, the rebellion was over and China had been officially declared a republic. Once demobilized, Mao returned to his education in Changsha, but this time at a less expensive teacher training college.

After obtaining his teaching degree in 1918, Mao took a job as a history instructor at a primary school. He also was inspired by the May Fourth Movement, a popular new social and political reform movement then sweeping the country. For Mao, as for many Chinese, the Revolution of 1911 had turned out to be a disappointment. The national government quickly fell under the sway of the rebels' top military commander, the autocratic Yuan Shikai, who forced the more democratically minded Sun Yat-sen into exile. When Yuan's sudden death in 1916 created a national power vacuum, regional warlords battled one another for control of China's countryside, leaving the nation more vulnerable than ever to foreign exploitation. Supporters of the May Fourth Movement sought to reunite their fragmented homeland under a strong national government and to set China back on the path of democratic and social reform.

Although Mao was drawn to the reformers' call for broad political, economic, and social change in China, by 1919, he was no longer convinced that Western-style democracy and capitalism were the best answers to the country's problems. Over the course of the next two years, Mao would devote himself to, in his words, "looking for a road"—a political philosophy through which his beloved homeland could be revitalized.[3] By early 1921, he had come to the conclusion that the ideological "road" he sought was socialism, a political philosophy associated with the nineteenth-century German philosopher Karl Marx. According to Marx, violent struggle between the different socioeconomic classes was the driving force behind human history. In time, Marx predicted, the "proletariat," or industrial working class, would rise up against the oppressive rule of the "bourgeoisie," or the capitalists, who exploited their labor. The workers would then establish a "proletarian dictatorship" over the capitalist classes in order to eliminate their influence in economics, government, and culture. Once the capitalists'

Pictured above from left, Chiang Kai-shek (1887-1975) and Sun Yat-sen (1866-1925), Chinese revolutionaries and political leaders of the Nationalist Party of China. Mao's Communists would overthrow the Nationalist government in 1949.

power had been completely destroyed, an egalitarian "communist" society then would evolve, in which private property ceased to exist and the building blocks of a society's wealth, such as factories, raw materials, and land, would be held collectively by all.

"OUT OF THE BARREL OF A GUN"

When 27-year-old Mao Zedong decided to embrace Marxist thought, he became part of a small but steadily growing number of Chinese socialists. In Russia, a radical socialist group known as the Bolsheviks had overthrown the former czarist empire's short-lived republican government in October 1918. Encouraged by the Bolsheviks' success, Chinese Marxists had formed small groups, or cells, in several major cities and towns by 1921. In July of that year, a dozen delegates from the various cells, including Mao as Hunan province's representative, met in Shanghai to found China's first national Marxist political party, the Chinese Communist Party (CCP).

On returning to Changsha, Mao immersed himself in labor organization projects for the CCP. His enthusiasm for the Communist cause soon won him election to the party's highest council in political and organizational matters, the Central Committee. By the mid-1920s, Mao had thrown himself into an important new project: promoting the United Front, the recently formed coalition between the Communists and the Kuomintang, or Nationalist Party. Founded by republican activist Sun Yat-sen after the Revolution of 1911, the Nationalist Party had been led by Sun's top military commander, Chiang Kai-shek, since Sun's death in 1925. The United Front was the brainchild of the CCP's Communist mentors in Russia, now known as the Soviet Union. The Soviets insisted that before China could be transformed into a viable Communist state, the regional warlords had to be vanquished and the country united—a task that would require the assistance of the more numerous and better-armed Nationalists.

Although wary of the CCP's radical economic and political ideology, Chiang Kai-shek agreed to go along with the alliance in return for Soviet aid for his army. In mid-1926, he launched a major campaign against the warlords, with the close cooperation of the CCP, which encouraged the Chinese peasantry to furnish Chiang's troops with food and supplies. During the campaign, Mao played a leading role in the CCP's peasant organization efforts. Deeply impressed by what he viewed as the revolutionary potential of the impoverished and embittered farmers with whom he worked, Mao concluded (in opposition to classical Marxist theory) that the peasantry, not the urban proletariat, would be the fountainhead of any future Communist revolution in China.

During the spring of 1927, with the United Front seemingly on the verge of victory, China's fledgling Communist movement received a stunning blow. That April, Chiang suddenly turned on his former CCP allies, ordering his troops to round up and execute thousands of confirmed and suspected Communists. Mao and the other CCP members who managed to escape Chiang's death squads were driven underground. Scattering throughout the Chinese countryside, they set up small bases, or "soviets," in remote areas. Aided by a fellow Communist named Zhu De, Mao established what was destined to become the largest of the various Communist bases in Jiangxi province, on the border with Hunan.

By the early 1930s, Mao's Jiangxi Soviet had grown to encompass much of southern Hunan; it had effectively become a state within a state. The Communists' ability to win over Hunan's predominantly peasant population was closely linked to Mao's radical land reform program, in which farm fields were confiscated from local landlords and redistributed among the landless masses. Mao's popular economic policies also helped him attract increasing numbers of local recruits to the branch of the Chinese Communist, or "Red," Army he and Zhu De organized at the Jiangxi Soviet. Mao was convinced that building an efficient and highly disciplined fighting force was essential to the ultimate success of the CCP. "From now on, we should pay the greatest attention to military affairs. We must know that political power is obtained out of the barrel of a gun," Mao had told his demoralized CCP colleagues shortly after Chiang Kai-shek's brutal attack on the Communists in 1927.[4]

THE LONG MARCH

In 1930, Chiang Kai-shek, having finally subdued the local warlords, renewed his campaign to annihilate the Communists. His main target was the biggest and most influential of the Communists bases: Mao Zedong's Jiangxi Soviet. Between 1930 and 1932, Chiang launched repeated campaigns against the Jiangxi Reds, but owing largely to Mao's innovative guerilla warfare–based military strategy, his troops proved unable to break through the Communists' defenses. Finally, in late 1933, Chiang sent an army of 800,000 to encircle the Jiangxi base, determined to wipe out the Reds once and for all. By the autumn of 1934, the Communists were running out of food and other critical supplies. Deciding they had no choice but to make a run for it, on the night of October 15, 1934, Mao and nearly 90,000 of his Communist comrades fled the Jiangxi base for western China, where they hoped to find sanctuary at other soviets.

For 370 days, Mao and the band from Jiangxi, along with a steady influx of refugees from other Red bases in south and central China, hiked 6,000 miles (9,656 kilometers) through some of their country's most rugged terrain to escape their Nationalist pursuers. Along the way they crossed desolate plateaus, two dozen major rivers, and nearly that many mountain ranges. This arduous journey came to be known as the Long March. Their grueling yearlong endurance test eventually would serve as a powerful symbol of the Communists' dedication, stamina, and courage. As it turned out, the Long March also would prove a critical turning point in Mao Zedong's rise to prominence within the CCP and the Red Army.

Mao Zedong rides a horse during the Long March. The Long March would prove a significant episode in the history of the Chinese Communist Party and helped cement Mao and his supporters as the party's leaders.

In January 1935, as the Reds' retreat from Chiang's forces dragged on into its third month, CCP officials met in the Communist-held town of Zunyi to discuss the best direction for their beleaguered movement. At the conference, Mao argued forcefully in support of the guerilla warfare–based military strategy he had developed in Jiangxi and for making China's vast peasantry, instead of its smaller urban proletariat, the chief focus of the CCP's political efforts. The party's top leadership previously had rejected both ideas. At Zunyi, however, the demoralized Communist officials finally were prepared to listen to Mao, particularly after one of their most eloquent colleagues, Zhou Enlai, vigorously championed his side. Although he would not be formally recognized as the head of the CCP for nearly another decade, Mao Zedong was now the party's principal policy maker.

Under Mao's determined leadership, the exhausted marchers pushed northward from Zunyi, finally ending their odyssey at a small Communist base in northern Shaanxi province in October 1935. By this point, disease, death, and desertion had dramatically diminished their ranks; historians estimate that no more than 7,000 of the original 90,000 marchers actually finished the trek. Selecting the poverty-stricken town of Yanan as his new central base, Mao immediately began devoting himself to winning over the area's peasant population with land reform programs and rebuilding the depleted Red Army.

TERROR IN YANAN

Mao would remain at the Yanan base for more than a decade. During that time, he led the Chinese Communists in two wars: first against a foreign foe—the imperialist armies of Japan—and then against the Reds' old nemesis, Chiang Kai-shek. Japanese troops had occupied Manchuria in northern China since the early 1930s, but during the summer of 1937, the expansionist Japanese Empire launched a full-scale invasion of China. That same summer, with China's independence at stake, Chiang reluctantly agreed to a Second United Front with the CCP against their common Japanese enemy. By early 1941, however, the uneasy alliance between the Reds and the Nationalists had all but disintegrated. Any incentive Chiang or Mao might have had to resurrect the shattered Front completely disappeared in December 1941, when the United States declared war on the Japanese empire and officially entered World War II (1939–1945). With the powerful U.S. military now on China's side, both leaders felt free to expend less energy on fighting the Japanese and more on strengthening their own resources in preparation for the inevitable postwar showdown between their two armies.

As World War II raged, Mao guided a steadily growing number of CCP recruits in building the Chinese Communist movement to record strength. By the mid-1940s, the Red Army boasted approximately a million troops, and nearly 20 Red base areas were scattered across central and northern China, with Mao's central base at Yanan the largest and most heavily armed of all. Sweeping land reforms similar to those Mao had instituted in Jiangxi, along with an innovative indoctrination campaign designed to instill Communist ideals in the masses through dance, drama, and song, had won the Reds the loyalty of many of the nearly 100 million people who resided in Communist-controlled areas.

At the same time that Mao was laboring to expand Communist influence among China's vast rural population, he also was striving to ensure his unquestioned supremacy within the CCP. During the Yanan years, historian Jonathan Spence notes, Mao "was moving on a trajectory that was pushing him more in the direction of dominance and power."[5] In late 1941, to consolidate his (as yet informal) leadership over the party, Mao began a "Rectification Campaign" to "reeducate" any CCP members who dared to stray from his political views. As part of the campaign, CCP members were ordered to study carefully "Mao Zedong Thought"—Mao's published political essays—as the fundamental statement of Marxist socialism as applied to China.

Under Mao's ruthless direction, the rectification crusade soon degenerated into a vicious purge of any party members whom he considered as a potential challenge to his authority. One of Mao's first targets was Wang Shiwei, a writer and devout Communist who had become a popular figure among the thousands of young recruits who flocked to the Yanan Soviet. Disillusioned with the corrupt regime of Chiang Kai-shek, Wang, like many youthful volunteers, hoped that Communism would bring a more egalitarian society to China. Once in Yanan, however, many volunteers soon discovered that the highest-ranking CCP members inevitably received the best food and medical care, whereas the lowly recruits were allotted only meager rations and no access to scarce medicines. When, to the delight of many of the recruits, Wang criticized these blatant inequities in an editorial for the local newspaper, *Liberation Daily*, Mao decided to teach the writer and his young admirers a lesson. At a humiliating show trial, Wang was accused of harboring "anti-Party thoughts" and sentenced to prison.[6] For months after the trial, regular and compulsory meetings were held at the base, at which the recruits were commanded to denounce their champion for trying to undermine Mao and the entire Communist movement. Those who resisted were subjected to physical and psychological torture ranging from whippings to mock executions. The Rectification Campaign lasted three years and resulted in the imprisonment of well over a thousand "bad elements," as Mao labeled anyone he viewed as a threat to his absolute rule.[7]

"THE PEOPLE'S GREAT SAVIOR"

It was during the Yanan Rectification Campaign that a full-blown personality cult of Mao emerged for the first time, a cult that eventually raised the CCP leader to almost godlike status among many Chinese. Viewing the personality cult as yet another way to bend the Communist movement to his will, Mao—although he preferred not to advertise it—was the movement's chief author, according to Chang and Halliday. "Every step in the construction of his cult was choreographed by Mao himself," they write. "He minutely controlled its main vehicle, *Liberation Daily*, using giant headlines like 'Comrade Mao Zedong is the Savior of the Chinese People!'"[8] It also was during the Rectification Campaign that giant portraits of Mao began to appear on government buildings and town walls in Communist-controlled areas and that the Maoist ode destined to become the Cultural Revolution's unofficial anthem, "The East Is Red," was composed:

> The East is Red, the sun rises.
> In China a Mao Zedong is born.
> He seeks the people's happiness.
> He is the people's Great Savior.[9]

In 1943, the success of the Rectification Campaign and the accompanying personality cult cemented Mao's control over the CCP. He was simultaneously appointed as chairman of all three of the party's top administrative and policy-making bodies: the Central Committee, the Politburo, and the Secretariat. Two years later, Mao's supremacy over China's Communist movement was further confirmed at the National Party Congress, held in Yanan in 1945, as World War II was nearing its end. In the introduction to the party constitution adopted by the Congress, party officials proclaimed: "The Chinese Communist Party takes Mao Zedong's thought . . . as the guide for all its work, and opposes all . . . deviations."[10] It seemed that Mao's victory over his fellow Communists was complete. All that remained was to vanquish his old enemy, Chiang Kai-shek, and bring the CCP—and himself as its top leader—to dominance over all of China.

3

Setting the Stage

In June 1946, less than a year after Japan's surrender to the Allies brought an end to World War II, full-scale civil war broke out between the People's Liberation Army (PLA), as the Red Army now was called, and Chiang Kai-shek's Nationalist Army. At first it seemed that Chiang's larger force would prevail. Then, in late 1948, the tide began to turn in what the Communists had dubbed "The War of Liberation." Bolstered by mass peasant support and ably led by Mao and his Long March comrades, Zhu De, Zhou Enlai, Peng Dehuai, and Lin Biao, the PLA managed to secure most of northern and central China. During the summer of 1949, Chiang began withdrawing his forces—along with all of the government's silver and gold reserves—to the island of Taiwan off southeastern China, where he eventually established a Nationalist government. On

The People's Liberation Army enters Beijing in 1949. As Communist troops march through the city, propaganda trucks like the one seen here attempt to whip up enthusiasm among the citizens. This truck carries a red banner with a photo of Mao in the center of a red star.

September 30, with virtually the entire mainland in Communist hands, the CCP Central Committee declared the formation of the new People's Republic of China with Chairman Mao

Zedong as its leader. The next day, Mao stood before a cheering throng at Beijing's Tiananmen Square. "We, the 475 million Chinese people, have stood up," the chairman proclaimed, "and our future is infinitely bright."[1]

THE GREAT LEAP FORWARD

Following the civil war, Mao turned his attention to the formidable tasks of rebuilding his war-ravaged nation and reshaping its economic and social systems according to his Marxist principles. One of his first acts was to institute a sweeping land reform program designed to transfer most of the country's arable land from landlords to the poor rural masses. In 1953, relying heavily on loans and technical assistance provided by the Soviet Union, Mao instituted a Five Year Economic Plan to promote China's industrial growth. By the time the plan ended in 1957, the country's coal and cement output had doubled and its steel and iron output quadrupled. Yet Mao was dissatisfied. He wanted the PRC to "leap ahead" of capitalist nations and even its socialist ally, the Soviet Union.[2] In 1958, he devised a radical program to expand Chinese industry and agriculture at a breakneck pace while also moving the nation closer to the Communist utopia envisioned by Karl Marx, in which all land and other property were commonly owned.

The Great Leap Forward, as Mao's plan was dubbed, was based on his conviction that China's huge population was its chief resource. To best exploit this considerable labor force while also hastening China's evolution toward a full-fledged Communist economy and society, Mao decided to organize the country's peasant masses into communes of approximately 20,000 persons each. On the giant communes, everyone would live in dormitories, and all property, including land, livestock, and farm tools, would be shared. To build the most efficient and disciplined labor force possible, Mao's plan organized the residents of the new communes into military-style work squads. Loud whistles and bells summoned the uniformed men

In this October 1958 photo, hotel employees build a rudimentary smelting furnace as part of Mao's Great Leap Forward. With this plan, Mao had hoped to raise the Chinese standard of living within 15 years by reorganizing the rural population into communes, but the program proved to be a disaster.

and women to the fields every morning at sunrise. "At the command of company and squad leaders, the teams move up to the fields, holding flags," a visiting journalist reported regarding one of the communes. "Here one no longer sees peasants in groups of two or three . . . going leisurely to the fields. What one hears is the sound of measured steps and marching songs. The desultory [aimless] living habits that have been with peasants for hundreds of years are gone forever," he noted approvingly.[3]

To ensure that the PRC's industrial output kept pace with what he expected would be its vastly increased agricultural output, Mao directed factory workers to put in long hours on the job, even exhorting them to sleep at their machines so as not to squander precious time commuting. Particularly concerned with stepping up China's steel output, Mao hit on the idea of supplementing factory production of the metal with small-scale "backyard" furnaces manned by already overworked peasants, as well as by teachers, office employees, and others. At his behest, scores of primitive foundries were constructed in schoolyards, village centers, and other sites across the nation.

Yet by 1959, it already was evident that Mao's revolutionary social and economic program had serious flaws. On the agricultural front, disorganization and mismanagement had led to widespread crop failures. Morale was low on the country's nearly 25,000 new agricultural communes, where peasants tried to cope with heavy workloads and the loss of their traditional, family-based lifestyles. On the manufacturing front, Mao's scheme to boost steel production with backyard furnaces had proved an unmitigated failure: The quality of the metal turned out by the crude smelters was so poor that little of it was usable. To make matters worse, huge quantities of precious coal had been wasted on the project, compelling many Chinese manufacturing plants to rely on wood scraps and sawdust for fuel. As exhausted operatives struggled to meet onerous monthly quotas, work-related accidents also became a pressing problem in the nation's factories. Yet despite all the waste, chaos, and human suffering created by Mao's radical plan, few Chinese spoke out against the Great Leap Forward. By the late 1950s, it was clear that those who questioned the CCP chairman or his policies did so at their peril.

THE PERILS OF CRITICIZING MAO

When Mao initiated the Great Leap Forward in 1958, the country was in the thrall of the repressive Anti-Rightist Campaign. Launched in the summer of 1957, the mass offensive was a direct response to the short-lived Hundred Flowers Movement, an earlier CCP-sponsored campaign in which Mao urged his fellow Chinese, particularly professors, artists, and other intellectuals, to offer constructive criticism of the young Communist government. Having persuaded himself that the criticism would be minor, Mao was dismayed when many people voiced grave concerns regarding his regime's policies. Resolved to crush any challenge to his autocratic rule, Mao turned viciously on his critics, branding them with two of the most undesirable titles in the Communist vocabulary: "rightist" and "counterrevolutionary." Between 1957 and 1959, at least 500,000 Chinese were labeled as counterrevolutionaries and rightist enemies of the people. Their punishments ranged from reductions in pay to being shipped off to forced labor camps in remote areas of the country where they underwent "thought reform."[4] A number of the detainees committed suicide; many others died at the bleak camps from disease, malnutrition, or overwork. Little wonder, then, that most Chinese remained cautiously silent regarding Mao's Great Leap policies, despite their obvious shortcomings.

Mao's senior colleagues in the CCP also were hesitant to point out the harmful effect the chairman's development plan was having on the PRC's economy and citizens. However, by July 1959, when Mao convened a special Central Committee meeting in the town of Lushan to review the Great Leap's first year, Defense Minister Peng Dehuai, the chairman's old Long March comrade, had decided he must speak up. A few months earlier, Peng had taken an eye-opening tour of his and Mao's home province of Hunan. Serious food shortages, he discovered, had developed in many of the province's rural communities. Thousands had perished from diseases caused or worsened by chronic malnutrition. Yet even in the face of widespread hunger, local cadres continued to exact large quantities of grain from the countryside to feed the massive urban labor force needed to fill Great Leap manufacturing quotas, which created deep resentment among the peasantry. The disgruntled peasants also complained to Peng of brutal and dishonest commune officials who relied on beatings to keep exhausted workers in the fields and who falsified crop yield reports when grain harvests failed to meet governmental expectations.

Instead of airing these findings before the entire Lushan Conference, Peng decided to present them to Mao in a personal note. Peng's discretion in approaching him privately regarding the Great Leap's failings, however, failed to soothe the autocratic chairman. Mao was enraged by his underling's audacity in daring to question his policies at all. A few days after receiving Peng's note, Mao had copies of the letter distributed to all 150 of the senior political and military cadres at the Lushan meeting. Then, in an impassioned speech before the assembled officials, he angrily challenged them to choose between him and Peng. If they supported Peng, Mao warned, then just as he had done when he led the Communists to victory against Chiang Kai-shek, he would go into the hills and rally the Chinese people against the government. "If those of you in the Liberation Army won't follow me," he added ominously to the military personnel present, "then I will go and find a [new] Red Army."[5] Jonathan Spence writes, "Confronted by this stark choice, not a single cadre sided publicly with Peng."[6] When the Lushan Conference ended a week later, Mao summarily removed Peng from all his governmental posts and placed the 61-year-old under virtual house arrest. His new defense minister, Mao announced, would be former Long Marcher and PLA marshal Lin Biao, one of the chairman's most zealous supporters.

ROLLING BACK THE GREAT LEAP

In the wake of the Lushan Conference, all of Mao's top colleagues in the CCP—including Liu Shaoqi, the CCP vice chairman and, since the previous April, president of the PRC—strongly reaffirmed their commitment to the Great Leap Forward. Over the next two years, however, the rural food shortages that Peng Dehuai had observed in Hunan in early 1959 worsened dramatically as bad weather and flooding decimated grain harvests in many parts of China. When the government nonetheless continued to requisition large quantities of grains from the countryside to feed urban factory workers, China was plunged into the worst famine in its recorded history. Between 1960 and 1961, at least 20 million people, the vast majority of them peasants, died from starvation or disease. By early 1961, to the relief of his increasingly worried colleagues in Beijing, Mao finally conceded that his Great Leap plan was foundering. He declined to take personal responsibility for the program's failures, blaming them instead on incompetent or corrupt local cadres.

As the 1960s progressed, Mao distanced himself even more from the Great Leap debacle, largely turning over the problems of how to end the famine and how to revive China's battered economy to Vice Chairman Liu Shaoqi and General Secretary Deng Xiaoping. When he had resigned the presidency of the PRC in favor of Liu in April 1959, Mao explained that he wanted more free time to work on his theoretical writings. (Since the presidency was chiefly a ceremonial position, though, Mao was not relinquishing any meaningful political influence by giving up the post. All true political power in the PRC derived from one's standing within the Communist Party.) Now, as Liu and Deng struggled to cope with the economic and human catastrophes created by his Great Leap policies, Mao composed essays on China's proper place in the Marxist scheme of world revolution and on the flagging revolutionary zeal of the current Soviet regime of Nikita Khrushchev.

A smiling Chairman Mao surrounded by students and teachers in 1959.

Under Liu and Deng's pragmatic direction, the Chinese economy was stabilized during the early 1960s as Mao's radical Great Leap policies gradually were abandoned. The massive rural communes were split into smaller units, peasants once again were permitted to grow some food crops on private plots, and governmental quotas for agricultural and industrial production were reduced to more realistic levels. In steel mills and other factories, worker productivity was encouraged through pay incentives and promises of promotion, which Mao had denounced during the Great Leap as rightist vestiges of China's old capitalist system.

MAO LASHES OUT AT SOVIET "REVISIONISM"

During the late 1950s and early 1960s, relations between the PRC and its Communist neighbor, the Soviet Union, steadily soured. The trouble between the two countries began in 1956, following the death of Joseph Stalin, the longtime Soviet dictator. Soon after the tyrannical leader's demise, his successor, Nikita Khrushchev, publicly censured Stalin for the brutality of his repressive regime and for the cult of personality that had grown up around him. Khrushchev's blunt criticism of his predecessor shocked and incensed Mao who, like Stalin, had relied heavily on both the violent suppression of dissidents and his cult of personality to build and maintain his own political power over the years. Khrushchev further angered Mao during the late 1950s by embracing a policy of peaceful coexistence between the Soviet Union and the leading democratic powers, including the vehemently anticommunist United States. When Mao openly criticized Khrushchev for relieving tensions with the West, Khrushchev

MAO FIGHTS BACK

Although Mao had given Liu and Deng nearly free rein in repairing China's broken economy, by 1963, he was becoming increasingly dissatisfied with what he viewed as their backward-looking and overly cautious approach. To Mao, Liu and Deng's moderate rural and industrial policies were a rejection of his own radical economic and social vision for the PRC. Adding insult to injury, he could not help but notice that the two senior CCP cadres were consulting him less frequently regarding the day-to-day running of the government. To help him regain his formerly paramount influence within the CCP and to revive what he saw

retaliated by ridiculing Mao's Great Leap Forward program. By the summer of 1960, relations between Moscow and Beijing had deteriorated so far that Khrushchev pulled all Soviet technical advisers out of the PRC.

In 1962, the Moscow-Beijing break became complete after Mao began openly deriding Khrushchev and his supporters in the Soviet Union as a clique of self-serving bureaucrats and "revisionists" who sought to rewrite Marxist theory to justify their retreat from true socialism. Mao accused Khrushchev and his "revisionist clique" of putting the Soviet Union back on the road to capitalism, with their emphasis on raising production levels through material incentives and their willingness to tolerate significant differences in income. By 1964, he was warning darkly that the PRC easily could fall prey to Khrushchev-style revisionism, unless the CCP leadership remained firmly in the hands of "proletarian revolutionaries."* Two years later, Mao would use this very argument to help justify the launching of a destructive and violent new political upheaval in China, the Cultural Revolution.

* Quoted in Philip Short, *Mao: A Life*, p. 523.

as the PRC's faltering commitment to Communist ideals under Liu and Deng's leadership, Mao turned to the man whom he had come to consider as his most loyal follower, Lin Biao.

Ever since he replaced Peng Dehuai as defense minister in 1959, Lin Biao had done everything in his power to promote Mao's stature and influence within the People's Liberation Army. To guarantee the PLA's absolute loyalty to the chairman, he first purged Peng's closest associates from the army. Then Lin launched an intensive political indoctrination campaign among the PLA officers and rank and file, which focused almost exclusively on Mao Zedong Thought. Soldiers were ordered not only to study Mao's leading political essays and speeches but also to memorize selected quotations from them. To make this assignment easier, Lin proposed that a handy digest of the chairman's sayings be compiled for the troops. His recommendation led to the publication in 1964 of what was destined to become the bible of the Chinese Cultural Revolution: a bound, pocket-size red collection of Mao's key political and social ideas popularly dubbed "The Little Red Book." That same year, with Mao's blessing, Lin initiated a nationwide campaign to promote the chairman's personality cult on an even more ambitious scale. As part of the new mass campaign, the Chinese people were urged "to learn from the People's Liberation Army," which Lin portrayed as the only top organization in the PRC that "truly fit Mao's ideals."[7] As part of the "Learn from the PLA" campaign, millions of copies of The Little Red Book were printed up and distributed to cities and towns across the nation so that every man, woman, and child would have the opportunity to follow the soldiers in studying the supposedly unparalleled wisdom of the "Great Teacher" and "Great Helmsman."[8]

At the same time that Lin Biao was helping to secure an untouchable power base for the party chairman in the PLA and revitalizing his personality cult among the Chinese masses, Mao also was beginning to reassert his influence within the CCP Central Committee. From late 1962 on, Mao repeatedly admonished party officials over the recent drift back toward private ownership of land, saying it posed a grave threat to the "revolutionary cause of the proletariat" by encouraging

LIU SHAOQI

Destined to be the most senior victim of the Chinese Cultural Revolution, CCP vice chairman and PRC president Liu Shaoqi was born into a middling peasant family in Mao's home province of Hunan in 1898. Fluent in Russian and French, Liu studied for a time in the Soviet Union before joining the fledgling Chinese Communist Party in 1922. Liu's long association with Mao Zedong began that same year, when he became Mao's aide in the Hunan branch of the CCP.

Known for his tireless efforts as a labor organizer, Liu was elected to the CCP's powerful Central Committee in 1927, shortly after the demise of the United Front between the Communists and the Nationalists. Seven years later, he fled the besieged Communist base in Jiangxi province with Mao and approximately 90,000 other Communists as part of the famous Long March. Liu continued his ascendancy through the ranks of the CCP at Mao's new base in Yanan in Shaanxi province, where Mao relied heavily on his Long March comrade's organizational skills in cementing his dominant position within the party leadership. By the late 1930s, Liu also generally was recognized as the CCP's chief theoretical spokesman because of a series of influential lectures on Communism he delivered in Yanan. After the People's Republic of China was proclaimed on October 1, 1949, Liu was appointed CCP vice chairman—the second-most powerful man in the new state after Mao, and the chairman's heir apparent.

the creation of a new capitalistic bourgeoisie (middle class) in China.[9] Even more worrisome than the resurgence of capitalism in rural China, he asserted, was the decline in recent years of fundamentalist Marxist values within the party itself.

By January 1965, Mao had imparted a new sense of urgency to his warnings regarding the party's flagging revolutionary spirit by claiming that "revisionism" had so permeated the CCP that even some of the organization's top officials were embracing capitalistic values and policies. (By "revisionism," Mao meant any attempt to revise or rewrite Marxist theory in order to justify a retreat from genuine socialist principles.) In a CCP directive issued that same month, the chairman cautioned that "people in positions of authority within the Party," including leading members of the Central Committee—the highest council in political matters—were taking "the capitalist road," although he did not identify the offenders by name.[10] If the party hierarchy proved unable or unwilling to cleanse itself of these revisionist elements, then a new "mass struggle"—in effect a second Chinese Communist revolution—might be needed to "rectify" the CCP leadership from below, he warned ominously.[11] Liu Shaoqi, Deng Xiaoping, and Mao's other colleagues on the Central Committee could not have realized it then, but the stage had been set for the most violent and tumultuous political movement in China's history.

The Cultural Revolution Begins

In January 1965, Mao had warned that "people in positions of authority within the Party" were betraying China's revolutionary heritage and taking "the capitalist road."[1] Over the next 10 months, with the critical assistance of a new inner circle chosen for their absolute loyalty to himself and his principles, Mao quietly organized a searing attack on a play by a Beijing historian and author named Wu Han, the first victim in his war against those he saw as his opponents within the CCP and the state.

THE CAMPAIGN AGAINST WU HAN

The campaign against Wu Han and his play, *The Dismissal of Hai Rui from Office*, began in early 1965 when Mao dispatched his third wife, Jiang Qing, on a secret mission to Shanghai to enlist the help of a radical journalist in writing a scathing review of the popular drama. Wu Han's historical play told the inspiring story of Hai Rui, a courageous official of the Ming Dynasty (1368–1644), who lost his government post after reproaching the emperor for confiscating peasant lands. Mao had long admired Wu Han's historical writings, and when *Hai Rui* was first staged in Beijing in 1961, the chairman had voiced no concerns regarding the play, although several members of his circle, including Jiang Qing and Lin Biao, had objected strongly to the work. Wu Han's play, they maintained, was a thinly veiled attack on Mao's widely unpopular Great Leap program of forcing peasants to relinquish their private farms and making them toil on giant agricultural communes.

At first, Mao shrugged off Jiang and Lin's accusations. As he was preparing for what would become the Cultural Revolution in late 1964 and early 1965, however, Mao concluded that denouncing the play and its well-known author could prove politically useful, for Wu Han was more than just a historian and a dramatist. He also was vice mayor of Beijing and the protégé of one of the most powerful political figures in China, Peng Zhen, Beijing mayor and deputy director of the Central Committee Secretariat. Mao had little liking for Peng. Not only was the mayor a close ally of Vice Chairman Liu Shaoqi and General Secretary Deng Xiaoping, he was far too independent-minded for Mao's taste. Peng, Mao groused, ran the capital city as if it was his personal "kingdom."[2] When Mao first decided to target the vice mayor, he was hesitant to have his name linked to any published attacks on Wu Han. Consequently, he entrusted his wife with the sensitive task of enlisting a journalist to expose Wu Han and, by implication, his direct superior, Peng Zhen, as counterrevolutionaries.

Eager to assume a more active role in politics and deeply interested in the contemporary cultural scene, Jiang was happy to do her husband's bidding. During the early 1960s, Jiang, a former actress, had become increasingly involved in the issue of how the CCP could best use literature and the arts to promote its socialist goals. As part of her campaign to root out revisionist tendencies in Chinese culture, she had become acquainted with the writer Yao Wenyuan, a staunch defender of Mao Zedong. Because Yao lived in Shanghai, far from Wu Han and Peng Zhen's home base of Beijing, Jiang and Mao agreed that he was the ideal person to fire the first shots at *Hai Rui*.

When Jiang approached the young journalist in February 1965 regarding the chairman's undercover project, Yao was enthusiastic. Over the next several months, he devoted countless hours preparing what would be a 10,000-word diatribe against Wu Han's play, secretly mailing drafts of the manuscript to Mao for his approval. Finally, Mao deemed Yao's assault on *Hai Rui* ready for publication, and on November 10, 1965, the critique appeared in Shanghai's leading newspaper. In his article, Yao condemned Wu Han in the strongest possible language. Denouncing *Hai Rui* as an anticommunist "weed," Yao argued that by glorifying a Ming official who wanted to return land to the peasants, Wu Han's play gave ideological support to rightists who sought to "demolish the people's communes and to restore the criminal rule of the landlords and rich peasants."[3] Consequently, *Hai Rui* must be understood as part of "the struggle of the capitalist class against the dictatorship of the proletariat," he asserted, cautioning that the play's "influence is great and its poison widespread. If we do not clean it up, it will harm the people's cause."[4]

Back in Beijing, Peng Zhen was dismayed by this unexpected assault on his protégé. At first, the mayor forbade local newspapers from reprinting Yao's vitriolic piece, but at the urging of Mao's faithful backer since Long March days, Premier Zhou Enlai, Peng relented and permitted the essay to be published in the literary section of the *Beijing People's Daily*. By burying the article in the paper's "Academic Discussion" section, Peng hoped to give the impression that the controversy over his subordinate's play was just a scholarly quarrel rather than a political dispute. But this was not what Mao had in mind at all. "For the Chairman," authors Roderick MacFarquhar and Michael Schoenhals note, "the Wu Han case was very definitely political."[5] To ensure that the debate about *Hai Rui* was viewed in this light, Mao made it known that he considered the play as an attack not only on his Communist agricultural policies but also on him personally. Wu Han wanted his audience to identify the Ming emperor with Mao himself, the chairman accused, and the virtuous official who lost his job for daring to criticize his tyrannical boss with Peng Dehuai, the former defense minister.

MAO BROADENS HIS ATTACK

By the spring of 1966, Peng Zhen was deeply apprehensive about the ongoing Wu Han controversy. Although Wu Han had apologized long ago for any errors he might have unintentionally committed in writing his play, scathing editorials on *Hai Rui*'s supposedly pro-capitalist and anti-Mao bias had appeared in a number of Chinese newspapers. Peng's apparent failure to spot his subordinate's offenses was bad enough, but Peng's reputation received an even greater blow in early April when Jiang Qing released the proceedings of a PLA forum on Chinese culture she had chaired at Mao's bidding. Chinese intellectual and artistic life, the report alleged, had become permeated with "a sinister anti-party and anti-socialist line which is diametrically opposed to Chairman Mao's Thought."[6] This trend could be reversed only by the launching of a "socialist cultural revolution," it suggested.[7] As Mao, Jiang, and the rest of the CCP well knew, Peng Zhen had served as director of the Group of Five, a CCP committee entrusted with policing China's literature and arts since the group's creation in 1964. The forum's alarmist conclusions regarding the dire state of Chinese culture made it appear as though Peng had been suspiciously remiss in his responsibilities as the PRC's cultural czar over the past two

In this photo, enthusiastic young Red Guards brandish copies of Mao's "Little Red Book" during a rally held in Beijing in 1966, the first year of the Cultural Revolution. Young students like these were instrumental in Mao's holding on to power after the failure of the Great Leap Forward.

years. Mao was tightening his noose on the mayor: "Politics," he was fond of saying, is simply "war by other means."[8]

Shortly after the release of the damaging report, Peng was summoned before a special session of the Central Committee. At the meeting, two members of Mao's loyal inner circle, security specialist Kang Sheng and speechwriter Chen Boda, denounced the mayor as a rightist who had repeatedly undermined the party and Mao Zedong Thought. At a follow-up meeting, which was chaired by Mao while Peng's longtime

(continues on page 48)

"COMRADE WU HAN, I APOLOGIZE!"

The first prominent victim of the Cultural Revolution was the respected scholar Wu Han. After Wu Han was accused of criticizing Chairman Mao in his play *The Dismissal of Hai Rui from Office*, he became a major target for student protestors. One of the young agitators, Zhang Yidong, later recalled a "struggle rally" against the historian that took place in his Beijing home and in which Zhang took part. Wu Han's story, as Zhang alludes to at the end of her memoir, had a tragic ending. After enduring more than two years of repeated struggle rallies and physical abuse, he died in prison in 1969 at age 60:

> It all took place in June 1966. I was fifteen years old and a third-grader in the Beijing No. 1 Middle School for Girls. At that time, the whole country was criticizing [Wu Han's play], *Hai Rui Dismissed from Office*. In the papers we read article upon article criticizing the play. . . . The more we read, the more enraged we became. . . . How could we stand idly by, doing nothing, if so many years after Liberation there were still people in the capital who attacked our Great Leader by innuendo?
>
> One afternoon, at the end of June . . . we suddenly noticed the students in the "Long to Be Red" schoolyard surging toward the gates, shouting "To Wu Han's home!" and "Let's go struggle against Wu Han!" Our hearts burning with rage, we too followed the crowd as it charged . . . to the entrance of Wu Han's home. . . .
>
> The place was packed with students. . . . A girl was standing on the steps shouting at the top of her lungs, "Down with Wu Han!" and "Whoever opposes our

Great Leader should have his dog's head smashed to a pulp!" . . . I don't know who opened the gates, but suddenly the frenzied crowd came pouring in. . . .

Wu Han was sitting on a couch by the window. . . . The students were throwing books around and spitting. . . .

I had been pushed into a position next to Wu Han. Looking at his kind, benevolent eyes . . . I couldn't help feeling sympathy for him. However, I immediately recalled that he had opposed our Great Leader, and, putting on a stern face, I asked him, "Why did you oppose our Great Leader?" He hurriedly shook his drooping head, saying over and over again, "I didn't oppose our Great Leader." . . .

Shortly thereafter, our school president and Party secretary arrived. They led the students in a criticism meeting in the courtyard, shouted a few slogans and left, leaving me and some other students behind to write slogans. As I was holding a slogan-covered strip of paper in my hand—not knowing quite where to paste it—a student outside the window knocked on the glass and patted his forehead with his hand, suggesting I paste it onto Wu Han's forehead. At first I didn't have the heart to do that, but, again recalling that we had to be firm . . . , I pulled the tea table in front of him out of the way with an air of indignation and pasted the slogan in the designated place.

Later . . . I happened to read in an article that Wu Han . . . had died under tragic circumstances. . . . A feeling of sudden discomfort filled my heart. . . . Twenty years have passed, and still, every time I come to think of this incident, I feel remorse. Having now at long last confessed of my great wrongdoing, I silently ask for forgiveness, hoping that in his heavenly abode, the martyred spirit of comrade Wu Han will have found solace.*

---

* Quoted in Michael Schoenhals, ed., *China's Cultural Revolution*, pp. 329-331.

(continued from page 45)
associate, Liu Shaoqi, was absent from the PRC on state business, the mayor's alleged treachery was further condemned and he was placed under virtual house arrest. One month later, Peng was officially ousted from all his government and party posts.

By the time Peng Zhen was formally purged in May 1966, it was evident that the powerful mayor was not to be Mao's only high-level target in what the chairman had begun to refer to as the Cultural Revolution. Although Mao failed to provide a precise explanation of the nature and aims of his new revolution, it was clear by the spring of 1966 that he sought nothing less than to cleanse every aspect of Chinese life—political, social, and cultural—of what he viewed as anti-socialist (and anti-Mao) influences. The same month that Peng Zhen fell from power, a number of other senior Party and state officials whom Mao suspected of opposing his leadership or radical ideals also were denounced and hauled off to prison. Among the most prominent of the purged party officials were the director of the Central Committee General Office, which controlled intra-party communications; the head of the CCP Central Propaganda Department; and Marshal Luo Ruiqing, a Long March veteran who was a member of the Central Committee Secretariat and the PLA chief of staff.

Luo, who had been noticeably unenthusiastic about Lin Biao's campaign to promote Mao Zedong Thought within the PLA, had been suspended from his military duties at the end of 1965. After months of relentless interrogations by Mao's henchmen about his allegedly rightist views, Luo had leaped from the top floor of the three-story building where he was being held. Landing feet first, the general survived the fall, but he injured his legs so severely that he was left permanently paralyzed. "How pathetic!" Mao remarked scornfully when he was informed of his old Long March comrade's botched suicide attempt.[9]

On May 16, 1966, Mao released a Central Committee circular announcing the dissolution of Peng Zhen's Group of Five and its replacement by a "Cultural Revolution Group" composed of Chen Boda, Jiang Qing, Kang Sheng, the radical journalist Yao Wenyuan, and several others from his inner circle. In theory the group reported to the Politburo, the CCP's top policy-making body, but from the start the Cultural Revolution Group was Mao's personal tool. Alluding to the ongoing purges within the CCP and PLA's highest echelons, Mao cautioned: "Those representatives of the bourgeoisie who have sneaked into the Party, the government, the army, and various cultural circles are a bunch of counterrevolutionary revisionists. . . . Some are still trusted by us and are being trained as our successors."[10]

As the Cultural Revolution gained momentum over the next several months, it would become increasingly apparent that the allegedly traitorous "successor" who concerned Mao most was none other than his foremost political rival in Beijing: the CCP's number two ranking member, Liu Shaoqi.

MAYHEM ON CAMPUS

Two days before releasing the May 16 circular justifying the ongoing political purges, Mao quietly launched the next step in his crusade to revive his radical ideals and once unquestioned sway over the CCP: rallying China's vast student population to his cause. On May 14, Mao's trusted security adviser, Kang Sheng, quietly dispatched Mao's wife to Beijing University to meet with Professor Nie Yuanzi, the CCP secretary of the philosophy department. The purpose of the secret conference was to urge Nie, a well-known radical, to publicly attack the university's president and party secretary Lu Ping, as well as other school administrators, for their supposedly anti-Mao attitudes.

On May 25, after being promised "high-level backing" for her crusade against the university administration, Nie, aided by several radical colleagues, composed a "big-character poster"

The caption of this 1968 propaganda poster from the Chinese Cultural Revolution reads, "Chairman Mao Guides Us to Progress Forward!"

denouncing the school's administration and pasted it on the wall outside the school's cafeteria.[11] (Since the PRC's founding in 1949, so-called big-character posters—giant wall posters with characters up to a foot high—had been a popular form of mass communication. This was particularly true during the Anti-Rightist Campaign of the 1950s, when big-character posters were widely used to attack alleged opponents of the CCP and to stir up the masses in favor of Mao's repressive movement.) While they might claim to be good Communists, President Lu Ping and other top-ranking school officials actually were rightists who sought to suppress Mao's new Cultural Revolution, Nie's poster accused. Students and teachers loyal to Mao, Nie challenged, must band together to "firmly, thoroughly, cleanly and totally eliminate" all "counter-revolutionary revisionists, and to carry the social revolution through to the end."[12]

As word of the inflammatory poster spread through the campus, students were outraged: They had been brought up to idolize Mao as the "Great Helmsman" and "Great Teacher," their country's supreme revolutionary hero and foremost sage. Inspired by Nie's summons to hunt down and suppress the chairman's enemies, students stopped attending classes to take part in giant pro-Mao rallies, poster-writing sessions, and humiliating "struggle sessions" against suspected counter-revolutionaries amongst the university staff. Destined to be a standard feature of the new movement, struggle sessions were intense and often violent denunciations and interrogations of persons suspected of anti-Communist beliefs or activities. During the Cultural Revolution, their main thrust, notes Lawrence Sullivan, was "to extort 'confessions' and wear down the individual's resistance to pressure. Accused of being 'rightists' or 'capitalist roaders,' the targets of these struggle sessions were cajoled and pressured to admit to their 'crimes,' admissions that had to be made again and again."[13]

When Mao, who was away from the capital at the time, was informed of the uproar Nie's poster had created, he shocked Liu

A demonstration held outside the Gate of Heavenly Peace, in Tiananmen Square, during the Cultural Revolution.

Shaoqi and other CCP officials by praising its incendiary message, which he asserted should be broadcast by radio stations throughout the PRC. In the wake of the chairman's endorsement of the strident poster, student unrest spread quickly from Beijing University to college and secondary school campuses across China.

Throughout the late spring and early summer of 1966, as radical student demonstrations compelled more and more schools to suspend their classes, Mao continued to stay away from the capital, moving from one secluded villa to another in central China. Dismayed by the spiraling campus unrest, Liu Shaoqi decided that the quickest way to stabilize the situation would be to dispatch "work teams" to the affected schools. Long an essential part of the Communist regime's traditional top-down approach to handling problems at the local level, work teams were special task forces organized by the CCP to oversee particular political movements or to fulfill specific objectives. "The powers vested in these ad hoc work teams were almost unlimited," observe MacFarquhar and Schoenhals, "working regulations drafted for them by the CCP center stated that they could 'detain, isolate for self-examination, take into custody, sentence to [labor under] surveillance or imprisonment' persons found guilty of 'criminal acts.'"[14]

In light of the high-level political purges and Mao's outspoken support for the inflammatory poster that had sparked the commotion on China's campuses in the first place, Liu Shaoqi was anxious to obtain the chairman's approval for his plan before sending out any work teams. When he and Deng Xiaoping flew to Hangzhou, where Mao then was staying, to ask his opinion on using work teams to restore order at China's colleges and secondary schools, the chairman was evasive, although nothing indicated that he disapproved of the idea. Never imagining that he was falling into a trap, Liu, after meeting with Mao, decided to dispatch some 10,000 CCP cadres to educational institutions in Beijing and to other major cities across the nation.

MAO TURNS ON HIS VICE CHAIRMAN

Friction developed almost immediately between the work teams and the rebellious students. When students refused to comply with the teams' directives to cease their increasingly violent struggle sessions against administrators and teachers and return to class, the work teams denounced the young radicals as being against the party. The students in turn condemned the work teams as "black gangsters" and "counterrevolution-aries."[15] After radicals forcibly evicted more than three dozen work teams from their campuses, Liu Shaoqi retaliated in late June by organizing struggle sessions against the students' leaders and arresting teachers who backed the rebels.

Throughout June and well into July, Mao remained silent regarding the government's handling of the rebellious students. Then on July 18, following a highly publicized swim in the Yangtze River meant to highlight his continuing vigor at age 72, Mao returned to the capital. The next day, Mao coldly informed Liu that the vice chairman had provided the PRC with "erroneous leadership" by sending in work teams to suppress the campus protests.[16] Mao had long argued that to keep the revolutionary spirit alive and revisionism at bay, it was vital to "set fires" every so often, and that, he was convinced, was exactly what the students were doing.[17] To underscore his support for the young protestors, Mao withdrew all the work teams and dispatched the Cultural Revolution Group to schools around the capital to encourage the students to continue their revolt. "Whoever does not join us in rebellion, let him stand aside! Those who want revolution, stand with us!" proclaimed Jiang Qing at a mass rally organized by the Cultural Revolution Group at Beijing University.[18]

On August 1, 1966, Mao convened a full meeting of the Central Committee for the first time in nearly four years, to discuss the new Cultural Revolution and how it had unfolded thus far. At the meeting, which Mao had made sure to pack with his supporters, Liu conceded that the work teams he had dispatched to China's schools in June had made errors in their approach to the student rebels. In his own defense, however, Liu noted that he had never been provided with clear instructions for how the Cultural Revolution ought to be conducted. The upshot, Liu noted pointedly, was that "even when you have made no mistakes, someone else says you have."[19] Mao's response to Liu's thinly veiled criticism of him was to write his own big-character poster entitled "Bombard the Headquarters." Since June, as Mao angrily accused in his poster, certain "leading comrades" in the CCP had been trying to suppress the Cultural Revolution and replace the dictatorship of the proletariat with a bourgeois dictatorship: "They have . . . encircled and suppressed revolutionaries, stifled opinions differing from their own, imposed a white terror, and felt very pleased with themselves. . . . How vicious they are!"[20]

Soon after Mao wrote his poster warning of the unnamed "comrades" in the CCP headquarters who were deliberately undermining the Cultural Revolution, the committee approved Mao's blueprint for the new movement, the Sixteen Points. Heavily publicized on national radio and in China's leading newspapers, the Sixteen Points described the "great revolution" as a movement "that touches people to their very souls." Written as a life-and-death struggle between socialism and resurgent capitalism, the Sixteen Points stressed:

> Although the bourgeoisie has been overthrown, it is still trying to use the old ideas, culture, customs and habits of the exploiting classes to corrupt the masses, capture their minds and endeavor to stage a come-back. The proletariat must . . . change the mental outlook of the whole of society. At present, our objective is to struggle against and overthrow those persons in authority who are taking the capitalist road, to criticize and repudiate the reactionary bourgeois academic "authorities" and the ideology of the bourgeoisie and all other exploiting classes and to transform education, literature and art and all other parts of the superstructure not in correspondence with the socialist economic base, so as to facilitate the consolidation and development of the socialist system.[21]

On August 11, a few days after approving the Sixteen Points, the Central Committee also rubber-stamped Mao's plan for reshuffling the CCP's top echelons, a reorganization that left little doubt regarding whom Mao viewed as the chief representative of "those persons in authority . . . taking the capitalist road." As a result of the revised party hierarchy, Liu Shaoqi sank to the eighth ranking position in the CCP, while Mao's loyal supporter Lin Biao was promoted to Liu's former number two spot, making him Mao's new vice chairman and heir apparent. Few in the CCP really understood what Liu Shaoqi had done wrong, notes Philip Short: "But nor did anyone try to defend him. For thirty-two years, since the start of the Long March, no one had picked a fight with Mao and won."[22] With Peng Zhen and other once-prominent CCP officials languishing in prison at Mao's behest and the chairman promoting mayhem on the nation's campuses, August 1966 hardly seemed a good time to start.

Mao's Young Generals

On August 1, 1966, the same day that the Central Committee meeting opened, Mao publicly praised a paramilitary organization from Beijing's Qinghua Middle School dubbed the "Red Guards," after the peasant militias that fought alongside his Red Army during the 1920s and 1930s. Earlier, the CCP work team assigned to their school had censured the Qinghua group for penning a big-character poster with the defiant slogan "To rebel is justified," a phrase coined by Mao in 1949.[1] Mao's show of support for the radical teens thrilled not only the Qinghua Guards but also the dozens of other Red Guard volunteer organizations that had sprung up at Beijing secondary schools and universities over the past two months. As news of the chairman's endorsement of the Red Guards spread beyond the capital, the fervently pro-Mao movement attracted millions of new volunteers, most of them teenage students from the nation's cities and larger towns.

Eventually encompassing some 20 million young men and women, the Red Guard movement would play a central role during the violent and chaotic first two years of the Cultural Revolution. Looking to the Sixteen Points for guidance, the guards vowed to assist their Great Helmsman in ferreting out and eliminating "those persons in authority who are taking the capitalist road" within the PRC, along with removing all vestiges of the so-called Four Olds: old thinking, old culture, old customs, and old habits.[2] In turn, Mao hoped to use the Red Guards to destroy those whom he viewed as his chief rivals within the CCP and to revitalize the PRC's faltering revolutionary spirit by egging on his "young Generals" to "set fires" at every level of the party organization and in society as a whole.[3]

MASS RALLIES AND "REVOLUTIONARY EXCHANGES"

Between August 18 and November 26, 1966, Chairman Mao authorized the PLA to organize eight massive Red Guard rallies in Beijing's Tiananmen Square. Sporting belted, military-like uniforms and scarlet armbands, millions of Red Guards from all over the PRC flocked to Beijing to attend the rallies. At the stirring revivalist-style meetings, Mao's "young generals" sang "The East is Red" and other Maoist anthems, chanted Maoist slogans from their Little Red Books, and listened with rapt attention as Lin Biao and other Cultural Revolution group representatives exhorted them to serve as their idol's revolutionary shock troops. The highlight of the rallies, however, was when the chairman, attired in a green PLA uniform to highlight the gathering's militant tone, reviewed his adolescent storm troopers from a balcony high atop the Gate of Heavenly Peace. At the inaugural rally on August 18, the huge throng in Tiananmen Square went wild when Mao allowed an awestruck

Chairman Mao waves to a rally of his supporters during the Cultural Revolution. Mao wears the armband of the Red Guard, which signifies that he supports the efforts of his young generals in rooting out bourgeois behavior in Chinese society.

female middle school student to pin a Red Guard armband on his sleeve. "Mao had found his new guerrilla army to assault the political heights," writes Philip Short. "A whole generation of young Chinese was ready to die, and to kill, for him, with unquestioning obedience."[4]

"I HAVE SEEN CHAIRMAN MAO!"

The ecstatic letter excerpted below was written on September 15, 1966, by an idealistic young teacher named Bei Guancheng and was addressed to Bei's colleagues at Shanghai's Jianguang Junior Middle School. Bei penned the breathless note immediately after seeing Mao Zedong at a massive Red Guard rally in Beijing's Tiananmen Square. Ironically, less than a month after he wrote the letter, on October 2, 1966, young Red Guards from his own school savagely brutalized Bei. A colleague of Bei's with whom he had had a recent falling-out reportedly egged on the Guards, who accused the 26-year-old language instructor of being a counterrevolutionary traitor. Just hours after the vicious attack, Bei took his own life.

> Let me tell you the great news—news greater than heaven . . . I saw our most, most, most, most, dearly beloved leader, Chairman Mao! Comrades, I have seen Chairman Mao! Today I am so happy my heart is about to burst. . . . We're jumping! We're singing! After seeing the Red Sun in Our Hearts I just ran around like crazy all over Beijing. . . . I could see him ever so clearly, and he was so impressive. . . . How can I possibly go to sleep tonight! I have decided to make today my birthday. Today, I started a new life!!!*

* Quoted in Philip Short, *Mao: A Life*, p. 543.

So that all his young generals, even those from the republic's farthest reaches, had a chance to visit the capital and to see him in person, Mao proclaimed that Red Guards could ride China's trains and buses at no cost. The chairman even ordered the PLA to make sure that the students were supplied with free food along their way. By the end of 1966, as many as 12 million Red Guards had journeyed to Beijing to draw inspiration from their leader in his crusade to end the corrupting influence of "capitalist roaders" and the Four Olds and to breathe fresh life into the PRC's revolutionary tradition.

With virtually all secondary school and university classes in the country suspended, millions of Red Guards also took advantage of their free travel privileges to visit Chinese cities aside from Beijing that had flourishing radical movements. To build solidarity among his adolescent storm troopers, Mao encouraged the Red Guards to seek out like-minded students from throughout the nation with whom they could "exchange revolutionary experiences."[5] Accordingly, Guards from across the PRC congregated in railroad stations, in public squares, and on school campuses in Shanghai and other well-known centers of radicalism to discuss Mao's teachings and to share ideas on how to identify and eliminate all threats to their hero and his vision of the ideal socialist state.

ATTACKING THE "FOUR OLDS"

The Sixteen Points stressed that Mao's economic and social programs could be fully implemented only after every remnant of China's pre-Communist cultural and ideological heritage had been expunged from Chinese society. Otherwise, the document warned, bourgeois revisionists would attempt to use the "old ideas, culture, customs, and habits of the exploiting classes to corrupt the masses, capture their minds" and "stage a comeback."[6] On August 18, at the first of the gigantic Red Guard rallies held in Tiananmen Square, Mao's new heir apparent, Lin Biao, reiterated the Sixteen Points' alarmist

During the Cultural Revolution, Mao's supporters sought to destroy all traces of the "Four Olds"—old customs, old ideas, old culture, and old habits. Here, banned books are being burned.

message regarding the evil influence of the "Four Olds" in a speech before the one million–strong crowd. Eradicating all vestiges of the Four Olds from China, Lin admonished his young listeners, was one of the first and most crucial tasks the chairman wanted the Guards to help him accomplish in his Great Proletarian Cultural Revolution.

Inspired by this call to action, the Red Guards enthusiastically took to the streets of Beijing and other Chinese cities to ferret out and smash the Four Olds. Waving copies of their

Little Red Books and chanting "Long Live Chairman Mao," the young zealots held mass demonstrations to demand that local names they considered as "feudal, capitalistic, or revisionist" be discarded in favor of new "revolutionary" ones.[7] "Among the names that became popular overnight for shops, streets, and buildings," writes Michael Schoenhals, "were: Red Guards, Anti-Revisionism, Anti-Imperialism, The East Is Red, Red Flag, Patriotic, and Worker-Peasant-Soldier."[8] In Shanghai, Beijing, and other urban areas, Red Guards also declared war on what they viewed as bourgeois fashion styles, including tight jeans, pointed shoes, and long or elaborately coifed hair on girls and young women. Guards harassed and humiliated hapless citizens caught wearing unacceptable clothing, often by forcibly stripping them in public of the offending shoes or slacks, and females with flowing tresses were marched off to the nearest barbershop to have their locks cut short in a more sensible, proletarian style.

Soon the Red Guards expanded their crusade against the remnants of China's pre-Communist past and the "bourgeois influences of the present" to include forced searches of private homes whose inhabitants were suspected of owning antique or foreign artwork, books, or other unsuitable items.[9] Thousands of objects that failed to reflect the socialist value system were confiscated or destroyed on the spot, while all gold and silver, precious gems, and foreign currency was turned over to the government. At first, the Guards confined their search-and-destroy missions to the residences of individuals with so-called "bad class" backgrounds, such as former businessmen or land-lords and their adult children. The Guards quickly broadened their attacks, however, to include the homes of writers, artists, teachers, anyone investigated as rightists or capitalists in earlier political campaigns, and even local party officials. Between mid-August and September alone, Red Guards smashed or burned a wide array of personal belongings from nearly 340,000 Beijing households. The destroyed items included everything from musical instruments to scientific notebooks, and antique porcelain to family photographs. Not to be outdone by their revolutionary comrades in the capital, Red Guards in Shanghai reportedly ransacked more than 84,000 households over a period of just 15 days in late August and early September.

THE CRUSADE AGAINST CHINA'S PUBLIC TREASURES

As the Red Guards' "War on the Old World" spread across the PRC during the late summer and early autumn of 1966, Mao's young generals moved from destroying privately owned artwork, books, and other cultural items to assaulting public cultural treasures. To frenzied cries of "smash, burn, fry, and scorch," brigades of hammer-, torch-, and rock-wielding Guards descended upon temples, monuments, libraries, and museums from one end of their vast homeland to the other.[10] In Beijing alone, nearly 5,000 of the city's 6,843 officially designated historical sites were ransacked. Taking advantage of their free transportation privileges, millions of Red Guards from Beijing, Shanghai, and other major centers of the movement took their Four Olds crusade to the farthest reaches of the PRC. Thousands even made it as far as Xinjiang province in China's remote northwestern corner, where they torched historic Muslim mosques belonging to the area's largely Uyghur population, and to mountainous Tibet, where they vandalized virtually all of the deeply religious region's more than 6,000 Buddhist monasteries.

In their violent onslaught against all vestiges of China's pre-Communist past, some Red Guards even attacked their homeland's most celebrated cultural icon: the Great Wall. Fortunately, the historic 2,000-mile (3,219-kilometer) barrier was never one of the central targets of Mao's shock troops. Nevertheless, Red Guards reportedly vandalized long sections of the ancient structure, in some areas hauling away large quantities of bricks and stones for local peasants to use in constructing roads, housing, and even pigsties. Although Mao gave the Red Guards virtually free reign in deciding how and where to conduct their War on the Old World, he did draw the line at letting them sack the Forbidden City, the grand fifteenth-century palace complex in Beijing that once had housed China's imperial rulers. On August 28, 1966, after a Red Guard group announced its intention to storm the famous landmark, the chairman authorized his trusted minion Premier Zhou Enlai to declare the magnificent 800-building compound off-limits to the young cultural warriors.

Aside from the Great Wall and the Forbidden City, probably the most widely revered cultural relic of China's rich past is the Confucius Temple Complex in Qufu, Shandong province. Construction began on the vast architectural complex in the early fifth century B.C., shortly after the death of Confucius, a native of Qufu and China's most famous educator and philosopher. Mao had long been vehemently opposed to Confucianism; he thought Confucius's highly influential ethical and social teachings were backward looking and elitist. It was hardly surprising, therefore, that Confucianism quickly became a major focus of the Red Guards' crusade to smash the Four Olds. Resolved to wipe out all traces of Confucian tradition from Chinese culture, society, and thought, the Guards confiscated and burned Confucian texts and vandalized temples and monuments erected in his honor. By late autumn, a group of Beijing Red Guards had resolved to make the 10-hour train journey from the capital to Qufu to destroy the most sacred of all Confucian sites: the Confucius Temple Complex.

On November 10, 1966, the Beijing Guards, assisted by local Red Guard units, stormed the Qufu compound, pulling down ancient statues, tablets, and columns and desecrating the graves of Confucius and hundreds of his family members. During ensuing raids, Guards managed to destroy a total of 6,618 registered cultural artifacts, including 3,000 books and nearly 1,000 paintings. The damage to the site would have been even more devastating if Cultural Revolution Group chairman Chen Boda—presumably at Mao's behest—had not sent an urgent telegram to the Red Guards on November 12, directing them to refrain from burning the magnificent temple complex to the ground.

After the Red Guards finally departed Qufu in early December, however, something remarkable occurred. Residents of Qufu carefully collected the fragments of the stone monument that once had marked Confucius's grave and hid them in their homes. They realized that they could suffer imprisonment, beatings, or worse if caught with the relics, yet in the end, the townspeople's devotion to protecting their rich local and national heritage outweighed their concerns for their own well-being. Nor were the people of Qufu alone in their courageous determination to preserve China's cultural legacy. In Shaanxi province, for example, residents of the town of Sigou secretly removed and buried an ancient bronze bell from a Confucian temple that had been targeted by Red Guards. In Beijing, fast-thinking Buddhist abbots managed to save their temple's historic gates by pasting dozens of posters of Mao on them, forcing the Red Guards "to choose between mutilating the chairman's portrait and seeking less troublesome targets," writes Dahpon David Ho.[11]

DESTROYING PEOPLE AS WELL AS CULTURE

While the Red Guards were waging war on Chinese culture during the tumultuous first year of the Cultural Revolution, they also were engaged in an increasingly violent campaign against tens of thousands of their fellow Chinese. The Guards' chief targets included the usual "class enemies," such as former landlords, business owners, and intellectuals, as well as anyone in positions of authority—from teachers and school administrators to local party members—whom they suspected of "taking the capitalist road" or simply lacking in revolutionary zeal. As authors Yarong Jiang and David Ashley note, in

In this photo taken on January 25, 1967, Red Guards parade an official through the streets of Beijing and force him to wear a dunce cap as a mark of public shame. According to the writing on the cap, the man has been accused of being a political pickpocket.

all areas of the country, rural as well as urban, these "allegedly 'bad elements' were subjected to humiliation, physical abuse, arrest, torture, and even death" at the hands of Mao's adolescent shock troops.[12]

It is impossible to determine just how many people were victims of Red Guard harassment and violence, but their numbers are estimated to have run well into the millions. In cities and towns across the PRC, the young generals dragged "bad elements" out of their homes and workplaces and paraded them through the streets in tall dunce caps, a widely recognized

"IN PRAISE OF THE RED GUARDS": THE *RED FLAG*, SEPTEMBER 17, 1966

During the summer and fall of 1966, Mao and the Cultural Revolution Group attempted to use the *Red Flag*, the *People's Daily*, and other Communist Party newspapers to drum up support for the Red Guards and to spur on the young generals. In the following excerpts from an editorial for the *Red Flag*, the author blasts the United States, the Soviet Union, and other countries, as well as Chinese "counterrevolutionaries" for branding the Red Guards as "destructive brutes" and "fanatics":

> In the Great Proletarian Cultural Revolution, which was personally started and is being personally led by Chairman Mao, the Red Guards have . . . become the path breakers. . . .
> Coming out of their schools and into the streets, the tens of millions of Red Guards formed an irresistible revolutionary torrent. Holding aloft the red banner of the invincible thought of Mao Zedong and displaying the proletarian, revolutionary spirit of daring to think, to speak, to act, to break through, and to rise up in revolution, they are cleaning up the muck left over by the old society and sweeping away the rubbish accumulated over thousands of years of history. . . .

symbol of shame and scorn in China. Many of the accused had to endure repeated denunciation meetings and struggle sessions at which they were subjected to intense psychological and

The Red Guards are a new phenomenon on the eastern horizon. The revolutionary youngsters are the symbol of the future and the hope of the proletariat. . . .

Different classes take different views of the revolutionary actions of the Red Guards. The revolutionary classes regard them as extremely good, while the counter-revolutionary classes look upon them as extremely bad. . . .

They have vilified the Red Guards as "young fanatics" and attacked their revolutionary actions as "violating human dignity," "destroying social traditions," and so on and so forth. . . .

"Young fanatics!" Invariably the enemies of revolution are extremely hostile to the revolutionary enthusiasm of the masses, and they smear it as "fanatical." And it is precisely what the enemy hates that we love. Not only must the revolutionary young fighters maintain their exuberant revolutionary enthusiasm, they must also further display their soaring revolutionary spirit.

"Violating human dignity!" The Red Guards have ruthlessly castigated, exposed, criticized, and repudiated the decadent, reactionary culture of the bourgeoisie, and they have exposed the ugly features of the bourgeois Rightists to the bright light of day. . . .

Like the red sun rising in the east, the unprecedented Great Proletarian Cultural Revolution is illuminating the land with its brilliant rays. Long live the Red Guards armed with Mao Zedong's thought! Long live Chairman Mao, our great teacher, great leader, supreme commander, and great helmsman!*

---

* Quoted in Michael Schoenhals, ed., *China's Cultural Revolution*, pp. 44-47.

physical abuse. At the sadistic mass rallies, victims typically were made to stand for hours at a time in the excruciating "airplane position," with bowed heads and arms raised backward, while their young captors cursed them as "venomous snakes" and "pests and vermin" and pummeled and kicked them.[13] Thousands died or were left permanently disabled as a result of Red Guard beatings; many others were driven to suicide by Mao's young troops.

Despite the terrible physical and emotional toll that the Guards' malicious behavior was exacting from China's civilian population, Mao expressly forbade local police, party officials, or the PLA from interfering with the young zealots' "revolutionary" activities. "Various of his remarks indicate that Mao craved a measure of catalytic terror to jump-start the Cultural Revolution," note MacFarquhar and Schoenhals. "He had no scruples about the taking of human life. In a conversation with trusted associates later in the Cultural Revolution, the chairman went so far as to suggest that the sign of a true revolutionary was precisely his intense desire to kill: 'This man Hitler was . . . ferocious. The more ferocious the better, don't you think? The more people you kill, the more revolutionary you are.'"[14]

As 1966 drew to a close, Red Guard violence had escalated dramatically and was now directed not only against "bad elements" in China but also at other radical mass organizations. By the late fall of 1966, many workers and peasants had formed their own local militant organizations to promote the Cultural Revolution. Bloody confrontations between Red Guards and peasant or worker groups often ensued when the young generals tried to force their way into communes, villages, or factories dominated by rival revolutionary organizations. Deadly power struggles also had erupted within the Red Guard movement by late 1966. Increasingly, the Guards splintered according to local allegiances or "class" backgrounds, with the children of "five red category" parents—poor peasants, workers, revolutionary cadres, Communist martyrs, and soldiers—pitted against the

offspring of "five black category" families—wealthier peasants, former landlords or businessmen, and accused rightists
or counterrevolutionaries. Neither the growing Red Guard
violence nor the social and economic chaos the disorder was
spawning in China, especially in its urban areas, seemed to
worry the Cultural Revolution's mastermind. At his seventy-
third birthday celebration on December 26, 1966, several
surprised guests later remembered Mao jokingly proposing a
toast "to the unfolding of a nationwide all-round civil war!"[15]
It would not be long, however, before even the Red Guards'
chief admirer would be forced to admit that, unless something
was done to rein in the young generals, the Communist state
he had done so much to create was in danger of falling into
complete anarchy.

Reining In the Left

On December 30, 1966, just four days after Mao toasted to the "unfolding of a nationwide all-round civil war" at his birthday celebration, massive street battles erupted in Shanghai, China's second-largest city and foremost industrial center. The violence, which involved several rival Red Guard factions and worker groups, when combined with widespread labor strikes, paralyzed the city's bustling port and brought all rail transport to a halt. By January 3, 1967, the most radical of the city's various mass organizations, the Workers Revolutionary General Headquarters, had commandeered Shanghai's major newspapers and was demanding the overthrow of the municipal government.

"SEIZING POWER FROM BELOW"

Back in Beijing, Mao hailed the resolve of the Workers Headquarters to purge Shanghai's government and party bureaucracies of all "capitalist roaders" and to "seize power from below" in the name of the revolutionary masses.[1] To demonstrate his support for the left-wing Workers Headquarters, Mao sent Zhang Chunqiao, one of the Cultural Revolution Group's leading firebrands, to Shanghai as his emissary. On February 5, 1966, Zhang and representatives from the Workers Headquarters proclaimed the establishment of the Shanghai People's Commune, the PRC's first worker-led (rather than party-led) municipal government. The new regime took its name from the short-lived Paris Commune founded by the Parisian proletariat in 1871. Although the Parisian workers only managed to maintain control of France's capital for 72 days, their highly democratic and socialist-leaning regime was famous among followers of Karl Marx, who greatly admired the Paris Commune.

As it turned out, the Shanghai People's Commune was destined to be even more short-lived than the Paris Commune. Just 20 days after approving its establishment, Mao abruptly withdrew his backing. The new worker-dominated regime, he complained, left no role for the Communist Party. The chairman wanted the Cultural Revolution to shake up the Party hierarchy and to bring the organization more in line with his own radical principles, but he never meant for it to make the CCP obsolete. "There must be a Party somehow! There must be a nucleus, no matter what we call it," he confided to Zhang Chunqiao. Free elections and unrestricted political activity might *appear* to be progressive, Mao explained, but in truth they were "utopian" and "reactionary" and would only lead to "extreme anarchism."[2] In place of the Shanghai Commune, the chairman called for the creation of a three-part "Revolutionary Committee" made up of veteran party members, representatives from the PLA, and the leaders of leftist mass organizations.

During the winter and spring of 1967, Red Guard factions and leftist worker groups, inspired by events in Shanghai, launched their own campaigns in cities and towns across China to oust local officials in the name of the "revolutionary masses." In many areas, clashes among competing organizations occurred. Widespread violence by the more radical groups against local party and government officials all but paralyzed existing political organs. To reestablish some semblance of order while at the same time reforming what he viewed as the PRC's overly bureaucratized and conservative political system, Mao decided to initiate a new stage in his Cultural Revolution, which until now had focused more on destroying the old than on building the new. In this "constructive" phase, three-part administrative councils, modeled after Shanghai's Revolutionary Committee, were to be established throughout China in place of traditional governmental and party organs. In March 1967, the influential CCP journal, the *Red Flag*, proclaimed that provinces, cities, towns, schools, and workplaces across the PRC should form revolutionary committees consisting of the heads of "revolutionary mass organizations," party members with impeccable revolutionary credentials, and PLA officers. The new "revolutionary 'three-in-one' combination" would be "the political and organizational guarantee for the victory" in the Great Proletarian Cultural Revolution, the *Red Flag* confidently declared, and would be an essential step toward the realization of the ideal socialist society in China.[3]

THE PLA STEPS IN

Establishing the PRC's new "three-in-one" political structure was to prove a considerably more difficult and lengthy process than Mao had anticipated. Party officials, hesitant to share their formerly unchallenged authority with mass organizations or with the PLA, dragged their feet in founding the tripartite committees. At the same time, fighting between and amongst various Red Guard and worker factions, each of which claimed to be the true representative of the masses, was costing hundreds of lives and bringing economic production to a virtual standstill in many of the nation's industrial centers.

In the face of the ongoing turmoil, the PLA found itself assuming more responsibility for holding the fractured People's Republic together. In theory, the three arms of the revolutionary committees were supposed to have equal sway within the new councils. In reality, PLA representatives dominated the committees in those parts of China where they managed to take root.

In addition to its prominent role in the new revolutionary committees, the PLA also was playing an increasingly important part in the deadly clashes that had erupted across China by the spring of 1967. Mao and the Cultural Revolution Group repeatedly ordered the PLA to support his young generals, the Red Guards, and other "true revolutionary leftist" groups over more conservative mass organizations in local power struggles.[4] Fearing that the nation would be plunged into anarchy if the ultra-leftists were allowed to run China's provinces and major cities, many local PLA commanders instead backed the least radical—in their view, the most stable and responsible—mass organizations among the various warring parties. In places where committees had failed to secure control, including Guangxi, Anhui, and Jiangsu, local PLA officials imposed direct military rule to keep extremist revolutionaries from seizing power and to restore order in the provinces' chief economic and population centers. Troops also frequently were stationed in bigger factories and agricultural communes around the PRC, "and it was largely due to the discipline enforced by the PLA that production in both cities and countryside was maintained during those turbulent times," writes historian Maurice Meisner.[5]

Nowhere was the determination of local PLA commanders to promote relatively conservative mass organizations over ultra-leftist groups more evident than in the city of Wuhan, a major industrial and transportation hub in central China. In July 1967, PLA Unit 8201, a local army division led by Marshal Chen Zaido, boldly disobeyed Mao and the Cultural Revolution Group by supporting the moderate Million Heroes group in their bloody contest for supremacy in Wuhan against the radical Workers General Headquarters. Ignoring Beijing's explicit orders to back the Workers Headquarters as the most "revolutionary" of Wuhan's popular factions, Chen instead sup-

TIBET DURING AND AFTER THE CULTURAL REVOLUTION

Although incorporated into the Chinese Empire in the thirteenth century, the devoutly Buddhist region of Tibet in southwest China was largely self-ruling for more than six centuries. Following the establishment of the People's Republic of China, Mao decided to tighten Beijing's control over Tibet. After Mao sent troops to occupy the mountainous region in 1951, the supreme Tibetan spiritual and political leader, the Dalai Lama, fled to neighboring India, where he established a government in exile. Eight years later, in 1959, Mao brutally suppressed a popular uprising against PRC rule in Tibet, torching scores of Buddhist monasteries and temples and reportedly executing thousands of Tibetans in the process.

The Cultural Revolution brought a new wave of religious repression and human rights abuses in Tibet, as Red Guards from Beijing and other parts of China, assisted by local radicals, launched a destructive campaign against the region's "Four Olds"—and particularly against its traditional Buddhist culture and teachings. The young zealots burned at least 90 percent of Tibet's surviving monasteries to the ground, along with scores of temples, libraries, and religious monuments. Thousands of Buddhist monks and nuns were imprisoned, abused, and murdered. Tens of thousands of civilians also were tortured or beaten, in numerous instances to death, for such "crimes" as practicing Buddhist rituals, voicing their spiritual beliefs, or wearing traditional Tibetan clothing or hairstyles.

plied the Million Heroes with weapons and helped them lay siege to their opponents' command center. When Mao sent two of the Cultural Revolution Group's leading radicals, Xie Fuzhi

The People's Liberation Army of China occupies Tibet in 1951. Today, Tibet remains under Chinese control.

Over the past five decades since the 1959 revolt, repeated demonstrations by native Tibetans against Chinese rule and against Beijing's brutal suppression of the protests have provoked widespread international criticism of Chinese policies. A variety of leading international organizations, including the United Nations, have urged the Chinese government to grant Tibetans the basic rights of self-determination and freedom of assembly, speech, and movement. During the spring of 2008, a violent clampdown by Chinese authorities on pro-independence demonstrators in Tibet drew international ire and sparked a new round of protests against human rights abuses in the region by the Chinese government.

and Wang Li, to Wuhan to confront Chen regarding his policies, the marshal's troops defiantly arrested Xie and assisted the Million Heroes in abducting and severely beating Wang.

Mao responded swiftly to Chen's mutinous behavior. At the command of Defense Minister Lin Biao, main PLA forces, including an airborne unit, three infantry divisions, and several navy gunboats, converged on Wuhan in late July. Vastly outmanned and outgunned, Unit 8201 surrendered without a fight. All three of the chief actors in the Wuhan drama immediately were whisked off to Beijing, where the disgraced Marshal Chen was stripped of his command and held for questioning, while Xie and Wang were given a heroes' welcome at a gigantic public rally in Tiananmen Square. The outcome of the Wuhan affair certainly looked like a big victory for the radicals over more moderate elements among the PLA, the CCP, and the Chinese masses. By the fall of 1967, however, escalating factional violence combined with an increasingly unruly leftist movement had convinced Mao to reconsider his stance toward his Cultural Revolution's most fanatic disciples, including even his young generals.

THE TURBULENT SUMMER OF 1967

In the immediate aftermath of the Wuhan affair, Mao's support of the most radical among China's contending mass organizations appeared firm, despite the concerns of many PLA officials regarding the disorderly rebels. At the end of July, Cultural Revolution Group members Wang Li and Mao's wife, Jiang Qing, presumably acting at the chairman's behest, publicly denounced army officers for "suppressing the masses," called them "revisionists," and demanded their expulsion from the PLA. In a fiery speech before a local Red Guard faction, Jiang even went so far as to urge leftist organizations to arm themselves against not only their opponents on the streets, but also against the "anti-socialist rightists" who had infiltrated the military.[6]

Aroused by Jiang and Wang's diatribes against counter-revolutionaries within the PLA, radical students, workers, and peasants began stealing arms from military depots and from rail shipments. Despite repeated complaints from the PLA, Mao refused to publicly reprimand the Red Guards and other rebel groups involved in the seizures. Indeed, recent archival research suggests that throughout much of the chaotic summer of 1967, the chairman was pressuring local PLA commanders to hand over guns and ammunition to Red Guards and to other radical mass organizations to use against more conservative rival groups.

By late August 1967, violence between the increasingly armed mass organizations and by rifle-toting leftist groups against allegedly "counterrevolutionary" PLA units had reached a deadly peak. Thousands of civilians and soldiers died or were seriously wounded in the fighting, with casualties particularly high in major urban areas, including Guangzhou (Canton), Shanghai, and Beijing. The spiraling violence seriously impacted communications, transport, and economic production. Basic consumer goods became scarce in many cities and towns. In the nation's capital, conditions were particularly unsettled. Spurred on by the inflammatory rhetoric of Wang Li and Jiang Qing, Red Guard groups launched daring attacks not only on PLA troops but also on alleged rightists in the top echelons of the central government. Although the radicals repeatedly proclaimed their devotion to the chairman, their bold anti-government offensive left little doubt that the mass movement Mao had helped to create was rapidly veering out of control. In early August, hundreds of thousands of young militants gathered in Tiananmen Square to demand that Beijing's most prominent "revisionist," Liu Shaoqi, be handed over to the people for public trial, something Mao was unprepared to do. Spurred on by rumors that he was a "big capitalist roader," Red Guards, to Mao's dismay, even attempted to storm the offices of his longtime premier, Zhou Enlai.[7] The final straw for Mao, as

On May 12, 1967, a Red Guard waves a book of Mao's writings in the British colony of Hong Kong, urging others to follow him.

far as the increasingly unruly "revolutionary masses" were concerned, however, seems to have been the radicals' potentially disastrous interference in the PRC's foreign affairs.

On August 22, enraged by the arrests of several PRC journalists in the British colony of Hong Kong, Red Guards came close to creating a major international incident by setting fire to the British Chancery in Beijing with gasoline bombs and then kicking and pummeling the fleeing diplomats. Around the same time, inspired by a vitriolic speech by Wang Li that derided China's foreign ministry as timid and reactionary, Red Guards staged a violent takeover of the ministry's Beijing headquarters. During their two-week occupation of the ministry building, the young zealots scattered and destroyed sensitive documents and reportedly managed to embarrass the Chinese government by sending insulting telegrams to foreign officials.

MAO REINS IN THE RADICALS

By September 1967, Mao concluded he had no choice but to bring the Red Guards and the rest of the radical extremists to heel, before the capital—and the entire nation along with it—descended into total anarchy. On September 5, he instructed PLA officials to do whatever they deemed necessary to restore order in the republic. The "revolutionary masses," in turn, were commanded to hand in their rifles and other weapons. They also were warned against interfering with the peacekeeping efforts of the PLA, which, the radicals were pointedly reminded, was "personally formed and led by our great leader Chairman Mao."[8] In mid-October, the Red Guards, who already had been stripped of their free train travel privileges the previous month, were ordered to return to their studies. Around the same time, Wang Li, the ultra-radical Cultural Revolution Group member and onetime hero of the Wuhan mutiny, was denounced for allegedly instigating the Red Guard takeover of the Ministry of Foreign Affairs in August and was hauled off to jail. On Mao's instructions, Wang's fellow radical rabble-rouser, Jiang Qing, publicly repudiated "Red Guard excesses" and all criticism of the PLA, conveniently forgetting her own recent diatribes against "anti-socialist rightists" in the army.[9]

As justification for the chairman's sudden reversal regarding the Cultural Revolution's most radical wing, Jiang and other members of the Cultural Revolution Group blamed the August upheavals on a newly discovered conspiracy masterminded by Wang Li and other "counterrevolutionaries" in the CCP. The members of the alleged "May 16 Group," they accused, appeared on the surface to be "ultra-leftists," but in reality were "counterrevolutionary rightists" who secretly hoped to put China back on the road to capitalism. Wang and his fellow conspirators, it was alleged, had cunningly promoted the factionalism and disrespect for all military and political authority among the masses, and particularly among the gullible Red Guards, that underlay the recent turmoil for the "ultimate purpose of overthrowing . . . Mao Zedong and seizing state power."[10] Jointly directed by Mao's inner circles in the CCP and PLA, the crusade to track down and punish the alleged May 16 conspirators quickly degenerated into a "catch-all weapon for wiping out any manifestation, suspected or real, of political dissent," writes Philip Short.[11] Over the next decade, an estimated 3.5 million Chinese would be arrested in connection with the May 16 witch hunt, and another 2 million "spies," "newly emerged counter-revolutionaries," and "bad elements," including many intellectuals and educators, would be detained in a parallel government- and army-sponsored crusade dubbed "the Cleansing of Class Ranks."[12] As a result of the two state-instigated terror campaigns, tens of thousands of Chinese were beaten or tortured to death or were driven to suicide. Countless others were exiled to bleak labor camps or to remote rural villages.

Despite Mao's repressive crusade to restore order, deadly clashes continued in some parts of China until well into 1968. Most of the fighting involved various Red Guard factions. After a particularly long and bloody spate of violence on Beijing's Qinghua University campus during the spring and summer of 1968, Mao officially disbanded his young generals in July. Red Guard groups who refused to dissolve voluntarily were quickly brought in line by heavily armed troops, often with substantial loss of life, with the death toll being particularly high in southern China's Guangxi province.

By the autumn of 1968, the violence had abated and revolutionary committees, most dominated by their PLA representatives, had been established in all of China's provinces and major urban areas. Determined to prevent the disruptive Red Guards from staging a comeback, Mao decided to exile the young zealots to the countryside en masse. By the end of 1969, the central government had forcibly resettled 4 million urban students to rural villages and communes, ostensibly to "learn from the peasants." The government-imposed relocation movement had few fans among the students or their peasant "teachers." "Many rural communities resisted relocation of urban youth who had no knowledge of, or experience in, farming, no familial or historic ties to their communities, and who, in many instances, scorned the 'backwardness' of villagers," authors Jiang and Ashley write. "Typically, students either ended up in state-run farms—often in underpopulated areas such as Mongolia, Yunnan and Heilongjiang—or . . . in some of the poorest frontier areas. Most were desperate to find ways to return to their homes and families in the cities."[13] Despite the program's unpopularity, 8 million additional students were sent to the rural areas between 1970 and 1976, the year of Mao's death. Not until 1979 did Beijing finally allow most of the so-called "sent down" youth to return home.

THE DEMISE OF LIU SHAOQI

While Mao was disbanding the Red Guards in the summer of 1968, he also was making plans finally to dispose of the Cultural Revolution's most prominent political target. When the chairman convened the Twelfth Plenum of the Central Committee on October 13, the meeting's central business was the formal expulsion from the CCP of "the biggest Party-person in power taking the capitalist road"—the former CCP vice chairman, Liu Shaoqi.[14]

At the plenum, the Mao loyalists Jiang Qing and Kang Sheng vehemently denounced Liu, who had been living under house arrest in Beijing since Mao launched the Cultural Revolution in August 1966. Intensive government investigations of Liu had revealed that he was a "renegade, traitor, and scab," who had repeatedly betrayed the Party and its socialist principles since as far back as the early 1920s, as Jiang and Kang claimed.[15] As punishment for his grave "crimes" against the party and the state, the Central Committee expelled Liu from the CCP forever.

After Liu's expulsion from the CCP was announced to the public in November, mass rallies were convened to celebrate the fall of the man portrayed as Chairman Mao's—and the Cultural Revolution's—most dangerous domestic enemy. As for Liu himself, the ex–vice chairman dropped completely out of sight following the October plenum. Years later, the Chinese government finally revealed that he had died in late 1969 while in state custody. According to eyewitness accounts, the elderly Liu's death was slow, agonizing, and lonely. Although his physical and mental health had been fragile ever since July 1967, when Red Guards stormed the Beijing compound where he was being detained and savagely beat him, Liu was kept in solitary confinement during the final year of his life and denied basic medical treatment. Mao's old Long March comrade finally died from pneumonia on November 12, 1969, in a squalid makeshift prison in Henan province almost two weeks before what would have been his seventy-first birthday.

General Secretary Deng Xiaoping—Liu's closest ally in liberalizing the PRC's economic policies following the disastrous Great Leap Forward and the second "biggest Party-person in power taking the capitalist road," according to the Maoists—got off considerably easier than his former associate. In his concluding speech on the last day of the plenum, Mao recommended that Deng immediately be removed from all his governmental posts but allowed to remain a member of the CCP. Deng, Mao implied, had been little more than Liu's puppet; he was never one of "the real decision-makers" in the bad old days between the abandonment of the Great Leap Forward and the revival of Mao's absolute dominance during the Cultural Revolution.[16] Instead of being hauled off to prison like Liu, Deng was exiled to rural Jiangxi province, where he and his wife lived under guard in a modest apartment and toiled in a nearby tractor factory for the next four years. The Cultural Revolution did take a tragic toll on Deng's family, however. In 1966, Deng's eldest son, Pufang, a top student at Beijing University, was left permanently paralyzed after he jumped—or was shoved—out of the upper-story window of a school building following a struggle session with a gang of Red Guards.

On January 1, 1969, a little more than two months after Liu's formal expulsion from the CCP at the Twelfth Plenum, the *People's Daily* declared in a New Year editorial that "victory" in Mao's "greatest ever revolutionary transformation of society" was close at hand.[17]

Final Years

In April 1969, the Ninth Congress of the CCP hailed the "great victory" of the Chinese Cultural Revolution and the forces of socialism.[1] Nonetheless, most scholars agree that the repressive movement launched by Mao in 1966 did not end in 1969, but rather lasted for an entire decade, only concluding with Mao's death. That is also the official judgment of the Chinese government, which has placed the Cultural Revolution's end in early October 1976, a few weeks after Mao's death when his widow, Jiang Qing, and three other powerful radicals were arrested for allegedly plotting a coup d'état. By the opening of the Ninth Congress, the PLA had brought the chaotic mass movement phase of the Cultural Revolution under control virtually everywhere in China. Yet many of the radical policies and ideals of the Cultural Revolution lived on until the mid-1970s, notably the authority of revolutionary committees across the PRC, the inflammatory political rhetoric against the "Four Olds," and any allegedly revisionist influences in Chinese culture and society.

THE LIN BIAO AFFAIR

Mao wanted to ensure that the PRC would continue to be guided by his radical socialist ideals even after his death. Consequently, at the Ninth Congress of the CCP, the 75-year-old leader took the unprecedented step of having Lin Biao, his right-hand man, formally designated as his successor in the new Party constitution adopted by the assembly.

Within two years of naming the CCP vice chairman and longtime PLA marshal as his successor, however, the ever-suspicious Mao had developed grave doubts regarding Lin's commitment to Mao's principles. Determined not to arouse the autocratic chairman's ire, Lin always had made it a point to agree with whatever Mao said, particularly since the launching of the Cultural Revolution in 1966, when Mao turned on many of his old CCP and military colleagues. When conversing with the chairman, Lin once advised a subordinate, "You should be passive, passive, and passive again." Yet, despite Lin's best efforts to remain in his superior's good graces, by the summer of 1971, Mao had begun criticizing Lin behind his back, complaining darkly that the marshal had been overheard expressing some opinions that were not "particularly proper" for the future chairman of the CCP.[2] Although the details of what transpired next are sketchy, Lin's son, Lin Liguo, fearful that his father was about to meet the same fate as Mao's previous heir apparent, Liu Shaoqi, persuaded the vice chairman to flee the country with him. On the evening of September 12, 1971, the Biao family and several supporters departed China on a small plane. They were apparently headed for the USSR, but the aircraft ran out of fuel in Outer Mongolia and crashed, killing all aboard.

Pictured, Chairman Mao with his right-hand man, Lin Biao, at the Ninth Party Congress in Beijing. Lin Biao would later die under mysterious circumstances, reportedly while attempting to overthrow Mao.

In the years prior to his death, the fawning Lin had been portrayed in the Communist press not only as Mao's hand-picked successor but also as his "close comrade-in-arms and best student."[3] Consequently, the fact that Lin was attempting to flee the country when his plane went down posed a potential public relations disaster for the Maoist regime. For months, Beijing managed to keep any mention of Lin out of the Chinese press. When the government finally revealed the circumstances of the vice chairman's disappearance and death, Beijing claimed that Lin and his son had been conspiring to assassinate Mao and seize power. Terrified that their counterrevolutionary plot was about to be uncovered by the authorities, the men had commandeered an air force plane and made a run for the border on the night of September 12.

Whatever the real explanation behind the vice chairman's sudden decision to flee his homeland in September 1971, the so-called Lin Biao Affair was to have important political consequences for Mao and his Cultural Revolution. First, with Lin gone, Mao relied more than ever on the moderate Zhou Enlai, his trusted subordinate since the Long March days, to help him direct the republic's foreign and domestic affairs. Second, it gave Mao an excuse to lessen the army's growing influence in the CCP since the chaotic late 1960s, and to return to power veteran party members whose duties had been assumed by the PLA officials who dominated the revolutionary committees. Last but not least, it discredited the Cultural Revolution among a large segment of the Chinese public. From the official inauguration of the Cultural Revolution in August 1966, Lin had been presented to the public as the radical movement's most devoted champion in the CCP and in the central government, with the exception of Mao himself. Now, Beijing was asking the Chinese people to believe that the general had been a counterrevolutionary traitor all along, just like his predecessor as vice chairman, the disgraced Liu Shaoqi. MacFarquhar and Schoenhals write:

> As knowledge of it spread, the Lin Biao affair had a profoundly negative impact on perceptions of the Cultural Revolution among all Chinese who had any pretensions to political literacy. For many who had accepted, if reluctantly or in astonishment, the early purges of the upper ranks of the CCP and the elevation of Lin Biao as being necessary for the reasons given by Mao and his CCRG [Central Cultural Revolutionary Group] lieutenants, the death and denunciation of the marshal were a profound shock. How could a man who had been at Mao's side for four decades, who had been the Chairman's best pupil and personally chosen heir apparent, have tried to assassinate his patron? More important, how could the all-wise Mao, who had detected revisionism

among so many old comrades, have been unable to spot Lin Biao as being worse than all of them?[4]

NATIONAL SECURITY AND SUCCESSION CONCERNS

In the wake of the Lin Biao Affair, Mao depended more and more on Zhou Enlai, his devoted associate and the premier of the PRC since 1949, in directing party and state business. Unlike the increasingly independent-minded Jiang Qing and the Cultural Revolution Group's other most radical members, Zhou was, at heart, a moderate and a pragmatist in his economic and political views. Urged on by Zhou, Mao, by 1971, had decided to embrace a moderate new foreign policy direction that stood in sharp contrast to the vehemently anti-West and anti-capitalist rhetoric of his wife and her ultra-radical associates in Beijing.

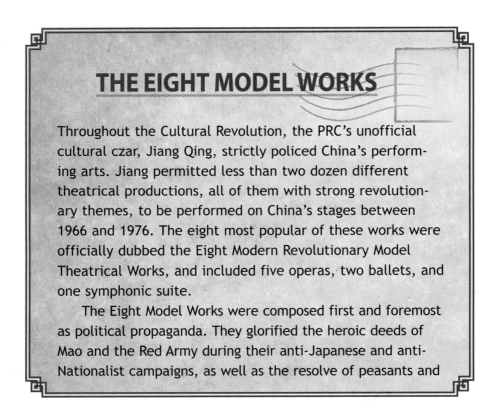

THE EIGHT MODEL WORKS

Throughout the Cultural Revolution, the PRC's unofficial cultural czar, Jiang Qing, strictly policed China's performing arts. Jiang permitted less than two dozen different theatrical productions, all of them with strong revolutionary themes, to be performed on China's stages between 1966 and 1976. The eight most popular of these works were officially dubbed the Eight Modern Revolutionary Model Theatrical Works, and included five operas, two ballets, and one symphonic suite.

The Eight Model Works were composed first and foremost as political propaganda. They glorified the heroic deeds of Mao and the Red Army during their anti-Japanese and anti-Nationalist campaigns, as well as the resolve of peasants and

Under Zhou's deft guidance, the PRC's new foreign policy program focused on developing closer political, economic, and military ties with the republic's implacable ideological foe and the leading capitalist power in the entire world: the United States. Mao's surprising willingness to pursue a relationship with the United States, symbolized by President Richard Nixon's historic meeting with the chairman in Beijing in February 1972, was rooted above all in national security concerns.

By the early 1970s, Mao and Zhou had become convinced that between the world's two leading military powers, it was the Soviet Union—not the United States—that posed the gravest threat to China's security. Relations between the USSR and the PRC had been strained since the early 1960s, when Mao accused Joseph Stalin's successor, Nikita Khrushchev, of being a revisionist, and Khrushchev retaliated by pulling all

workers to free their society from the influence of landlords and other capitalist exploiters after the PRC's founding in 1949. When President Nixon and First Lady Pat Nixon visited Beijing in February 1972, Jiang Qing accompanied them to a performance of the model ballet *Red Detachment of Women*. The lavishly produced story about a young peasant woman who joins the Red Army and becomes an ardent Communist featured ballerinas in military-style tunics and red armbands pirouetting with rifles.

Until Mao's death and the arrest of the Gang of Four in 1976, the Eight Model Works were performed in thousands of theaters across the PRC. Recorded versions also were broadcast repeatedly on China's state-controlled television network. It has been estimated that over the course of the Cultural Revolution, the average Chinese citizen watched each one of the Eight Model Works at least twice a year.

Soviet technical advisers out of China. During the mid-1960s, Sino-Soviet relations soured further as belligerent Red Guards humiliated and threatened Russian diplomats and their families in Beijing, and Moscow publicly derided the guards and the entire Cultural Revolution as fanatical and irresponsible. In 1969, the escalating tensions between the two nations erupted into armed conflict, with Russian and Chinese troops clashing over disputed sections of the Sino-Soviet border. Genuinely worried about the possibility of a Soviet nuclear attack on China in the wake of the border skirmishes, Mao and his top foreign policy adviser turned to the United States, the one country powerful enough to serve as a counterweight to the PRC's increasingly hostile neighbor.

Aside from his anxiety regarding China's neighbor to the north, Mao had another chief concern during the early 1970s—the question of who should succeed him as CCP chairman now that Lin Biao was no longer in the picture. Shortly after Mao's highly publicized meeting with President Nixon in 1972, the 78-year-old leader suffered an apparent stroke, and Premier Zhou Enlai, widely viewed as the most qualified person within the central government to succeed the ailing chairman, was diagnosed with a fatal form of cancer. In early 1973, with Zhou's encouragement, Mao brought the former general secretary of the CCP, Deng Xiaoping, from his four-year-long exile in rural Jiangxi to serve as Zhou's vice premier and, presumably, to be groomed as his successor. Mao defended his surprising "rehabilitation" of the disgraced general secretary by asserting that Deng, despite his past errors, was "politically and ideologically astute" and that he possessed "rare talent."[5] A shrewdly worded letter Deng recently had sent to Mao apologizing for his "mistakes" and praising the Cultural Revolution as "an immense monster-revealing mirror" that had exposed many "swindlers" within the CCP and government undoubtedly also helped Deng's cause with the chairman.[6] (In the Chinese Communist Party vocabulary, the term "rehabilitation" meant the reinstatement of formerly disgraced CCP, government, or military officials.)

DENG XIAOPING AND THE GANG OF FOUR

Although Mao relied more on Zhou's assistance and advice in political and military matters after Lin Biao's death, he continued to allow Jiang Qing and her radical associates in Beijing to have a great deal of influence in the ideological and cultural spheres. Throughout the first half of the 1970s, Jiang and her three closest radical cohorts, all together labeled the "Gang of Four" by their critics, dominated the party newspapers and journals and controlled which operas, films, and other cultural works could be produced within the PRC. Keenly aware that Mao counted on them to keep the leftist ideals of his fading Cultural Revolution alive, the Gang of Four had hoped that the chairman would select one of them as his new heir apparent when Zhou fell ill. Consequently, Deng Xiaoping's rehabilitation was a bitter blow to Jiang and her radical clique, which included Wu Han's old nemesis, Yao Wenyuan; veteran CCP propagandist Zhang Chunqiao; and Wang Hongwen, a former Red Guard leader who had been elected to the Central Committee in the late 1960s at Mao's behest. (Two important Cultural Revolution leaders who were not part of the Gang were Chen Boda, who was purged from the CCP in 1970 for his alleged ties to the disgraced Lin Biao; and Kang Sheng, who served as an adviser to Jiang until his death from cancer in 1975.)

Following his return to Beijing, Deng focused on increasing China's industrial output, which had plummeted during the Cultural Revolution's chaotic early years. In an obvious jab at the Gang of Four, Deng maintained that the PRC's successful development as an industrial power depended far more on expertise and efficiency than on ideological purity within the CCP and within Chinese society as a whole. Deng's emphasis on practical efficacy over socialist ideology in setting the PRC's economic policy infuriated Jiang and her faction, and they conspired to turn Mao against his old Long March comrade. It was not until after Zhou Enlai's death from cancer in January 1976, however, that the Gang of Four was able to persuade the chairman to dismiss Deng for a second time.

Mao's second break with Deng came on the heels of an extraordinary and spontaneous showing of popular support for Zhou Enlai and, by implication, for his close associate, Deng Xiaoping, as well as disdain for the Gang of Four. On

ZHOU ENLAI: LOYAL SUBORDINATE AND MASTER DIPLOMAT

Astute, charming, and unfailingly loyal, Zhou Enlai was one of Mao Zedong's most valued subordinates. Although it was Zhou's reputation as a political moderate that seems to have most endeared him to the Chinese public, during the height of the Cultural Revolution, Zhou was heavily implicated in the purge and brutal inquisition of hundreds of senior CCP members. Indeed, the fact that Zhou, unlike the vast majority of top CCP officials, managed to survive the Cultural Revolution unscathed was likely linked to his willingness to do whatever Mao demanded during the repressive movement—including denouncing and persecuting several longtime colleagues, such as Mao's Great Leap Forward critic Peng Dehuai, who eventually died from the vicious beatings he suffered at the hands of government interrogators and Red Guards during the late 1960s.

From the founding of the PRC in 1949 until late 1975, when declining health compelled his retirement from the government at age 77, Zhou served as China's premier, mak-

April 4, a day when Chinese traditionally pay respect to the dead, tens of thousands of mourners gathered in Beijing's Tiananmen Square to leave wreaths, cards, and posters in honor of Zhou. Along with eulogizing the late political leader, some of the posters contained derogatory poems about the "mad empress," Jiang Qing, and the other "wolves and jackals" in the Gang of Four.[7] When the crowds returned to the square on the morning of April 5 and discovered that all their

ing him the de facto director of the country's international affairs for more than three decades. A shrewd and patient negotiator, Zhou enjoyed numerous foreign policy successes in Asia and Africa over the years. Without question, however, Zhou's greatest diplomatic triumph was negotiating the thaw with the capitalist West, and particularly the United States, during the early 1970s.

Zhou's so-called ping pong diplomacy, in which the Chinese government reached out to its old enemy through Sino-American table-tennis exhibitions, paved the way for his secret negotiations with Richard Nixon's national security adviser, Henry Kissinger, in Beijing in 1971. When Nixon agreed to travel to Beijing to meet Mao in person in February 1972, Zhou assumed personal charge of planning the historic state visit and met extensively with the American president during his time in the PRC. Zhou's skills as a diplomat were particularly evident in the Shanghai Communiqué, signed by Nixon and himself on February 27, 1972. Recognizing that the Chinese and American governments held many incompatible positions that prevented them from normalizing diplomatic relations, Zhou suggested an innovative format for the communiqué in which each side expressed its views on divisive issues such as the Vietnam War (1959-1975) in separate paragraphs.

A propaganda poster depicting the fall of the "Gang of Four"—the high officials blamed for the worst excesses of the Cultural Revolution after Mao's death. In this poster, the four are shown impaled and burning, their human heads on the bodies of animals. From left to right, they are Yao Wenyuan, Wang Hongwen, Zhang Chunqiao, and Mao's widow, Jiang Qing.

wreaths and posters had been removed during the night, angry confrontations erupted between some of the mourners and the police. Although the police and state militia swiftly quashed the Tiananmen protest, the chairman was shaken by the unexpected popular outburst. Blaming Deng Xiaoping for what they characterized as a dangerous counterrevolutionary incident, Jiang Qing and her inner circle convinced Mao to remove Deng from all his government posts at once, although they failed to persuade the chairman to expel their rival from the CCP.

THE END OF MAO AND OF
THE CULTURAL REVOLUTION

Shortly after the Tiananmen Square incident, Mao appointed a new vice premier to replace Deng, an obscure party official from Hunan province named Hua Guofeng. "This remarkable promotion transformed the previously almost unknown Hua into Mao's probable successor," writes Jonathan Spence. "Though an odd and risky decision, the appointment of Hua was a deliberate compromise, to balance off Deng Xiaoping supporters against those of Jiang Qing," Spence asserts.[8] Hua, who had risen rapidly in the party during the tumultuous early years of the Cultural Revolution, had impeccable revolutionary credentials. Nonetheless, he was less stridently leftist than the controversial Gang of Four, from whom he kept a cautious distance.

Over the next few months following Hua's appointment, Mao's health declined steadily. On September 2, he suffered a massive heart attack. A week later, on September 9, 1976, the 82-year-old leader died. Flanked by the Gang of Four, Hua Guofeng delivered the eulogy at a mass memorial held in Tiananmen Square on September 18. Since Hua was a relatively unknown Beijing outsider, Jiang Qing and her radical cohorts felt confident that leadership of the CCP and the republic was finally within their grasp. Instead, just three weeks later, on October 6, Hua, backed by the PLA, had Jiang Qing, Yao Wenyuan, Zhang Chunqiao, and Wang Hongwen arrested as counterrevolutionary traitors and thrown into jail. Now that the radical Gang of Four had been silenced for good, there could be little doubt that the Cultural Revolution, of which they had been the most powerful surviving champions, was finally over.

The Cultural Revolution's Legacy

Following the Gang of Four's imprisonment, Hua Guofeng moved quickly to establish his supremacy within the CCP and the central government. Soon, however, Hua's authority was being challenged by Deng Xiaoping, whose supporters pressured Hua into reinstating Deng in his former posts as vice premier, vice chairman of the Central Committee, and chief of the General Staff of the PLA in July 1977. Over the next two and a half years, Deng gradually built his influence within the top echelons of the Chinese Communist Party. By 1980, Hua was sidelined completely.

REPUDIATING THE CULTURAL REVOLUTION

Once in power, Deng immediately set out to repair what he viewed as the enormous damage the Cultural Revolution had done to the authority and prestige of the Chinese Communist Party. To revitalize the ailing party, he reinstated scores of veterans who had been purged as revisionists or bourgeois bureaucrats, phased out the PLA-dominated Revolutionary Committees, and called for the official rehabilitation of two of the Cultural Revolution's most prominent victims: the late Liu Shaoqi and the former defense minister Peng Dehuai.

In December 1980, Deng had the Gang of Four put on trial for their role in the Cultural Revolution's deadly excesses. The trial, which was heavily covered in the state-controlled media, resulted in the conviction of all four defendants. Wang Hongwen and Yao Wenyuan received life and 20 years in prison, respectively, while Jiang Qing and Zhang Chunqiao were sentenced to death (later commuted to life in prison). Jiang, who insisted throughout the trial that she merely had been obeying Mao's orders, committed suicide in prison in 1991 at the age of 77.

Although the Gang of Four got their just deserts, authors MacFarquhar and Schoenhals contend that

> the majority of people who committed crimes during the Cultural Revolution did not. Reportedly, some in the CCP's Organization Department wanted a drastic weeding out of guilty party cadres, but that would have involved a massive purge at a time when Deng wanted to emphasize harmony and turn the country away from political struggle.... An attempt was made to ensure that former Red Guards attempting to enter or reenter universities had not been guilty of murder or assault, but how successfully this distinction was drawn is uncertain.[1]

After the conclusion of the highly publicized trial, Deng worried that something more needed to be done to repair the party's battered image among the Chinese public. The Chinese people, he decided, needed an official explanation for how the CCP could have allowed a movement as destructive as the Cultural Revolution to occur in the first place.

The Central Committee's official account of the Cultural Revolution was presented in a carefully worded resolution issued on July 1, 1981, the Chinese Communist Party's sixtieth anniversary. The Cultural Revolution, it declared, was "initiated and led by Comrade Mao Zedong." Although Mao was "a great Marxist, proletarian revolutionary, . . . and general," late in his illustrious career he made the tragic blunder of imagining that "counterrevolutionary revisionists" had infiltrated the party and government, the resolution went on. Mao's irrespon-

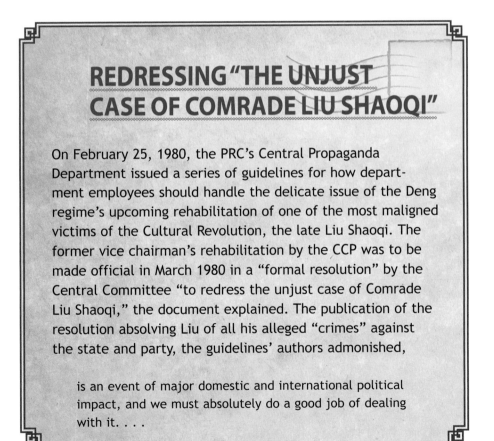

REDRESSING "THE UNJUST CASE OF COMRADE LIU SHAOQI"

On February 25, 1980, the PRC's Central Propaganda Department issued a series of guidelines for how department employees should handle the delicate issue of the Deng regime's upcoming rehabilitation of one of the most maligned victims of the Cultural Revolution, the late Liu Shaoqi. The former vice chairman's rehabilitation by the CCP was to be made official in March 1980 in a "formal resolution" by the Central Committee "to redress the unjust case of Comrade Liu Shaoqi," the document explained. The publication of the resolution absolving Liu of all his alleged "crimes" against the state and party, the guidelines' authors admonished,

> is an event of major domestic and international political impact, and we must absolutely do a good job of dealing with it. . . .

sible allegations and policy of mobilizing the masses to carry out his misguided "revolution" had led to 10 years of terror and chaos: the "most severe setback and the heaviest losses suffered by the Party, the state, and the people since the founding of the People's Republic." Nonetheless, the Central Committee placed the blame for the movement's worst excesses not on Mao, but rather on two small yet powerful political cliques, one led by Lin Biao and the other by Jiang Qing. "Taking advantage of Comrade Mao Zedong's errors," the resolution asserted, they "committed many crimes behind his back."[2]

In their account, the Central Committee was careful to point out that the late chairman's many vital contributions to

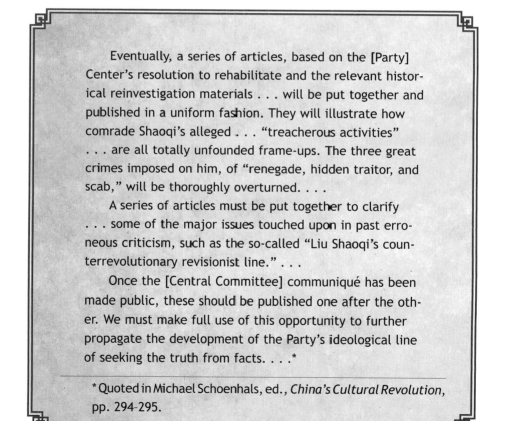

Eventually, a series of articles, based on the [Party] Center's resolution to rehabilitate and the relevant historical reinvestigation materials . . . will be put together and published in a uniform fashion. They will illustrate how comrade Shaoqi's alleged . . . "treacherous activities" . . . are all totally unfounded frame-ups. The three great crimes imposed on him, of "renegade, hidden traitor, and scab," will be thoroughly overturned. . . .

A series of articles must be put together to clarify . . . some of the major issues touched upon in past erroneous criticism, such as the so-called "Liu Shaoqi's counterrevolutionary revisionist line." . . .

Once the [Central Committee] communiqué has been made public, these should be published one after the other. We must make full use of this opportunity to further propagate the development of the Party's ideological line of seeking the truth from facts. . . .*

* Quoted in Michael Schoenhals, ed., *China's Cultural Revolution*, pp. 294–295.

In January 1981, Mao's widow, Jiang Qing, was put on trial at the Supreme People's Court in Beijing. Although initially condemned to death, her sentence was later suspended so she might "reform through labor."

the People's Republic far outweighed the unfortunate mistakes of his last decade in office. The CCP's top echelon recognized that "the legitimacy of the party still rested heavily on Mao's revolutionary achievements," note MacFarquhar and Schoenhals. As Deng privately observed, "discrediting" the chief hero of the Chinese Revolution and founder of the PRC "would mean discrediting our Party and state."[3]

"TO GET RICH IS GLORIOUS"

From his return to Beijing in 1977 until ill health compelled him to retire from the government nearly two decades later, Deng strengthened the PRC and its leadership by promoting the nation's economic development. Many of the PRC's neighbors in East Asia, including Japan, South Korea, Taiwan, Singapore, and Hong Kong, had experienced tremendous economic expansion in the 1960s and 1970s, while strife-ridden China's economy had stagnated. For Deng and other high-ranking party officials, note MacFarquhar and Schoenhals, "the message was clear: they had to embark upon a policy of rapid economic growth to make up for lost time and to relegitimize CCP rule."[4]

During the Cultural Revolution, Deng had been reproached for his emphasis on pragmatism over political ideology in policymaking. "The color of the cat does not matter," Deng liked to say, "as long as it catches mice."[5] Breaking with radical Maoist tradition in order to accelerate China's economic development, Deng opened the country to foreign trade and investment, dismantled agricultural communes, instituted cash incentives to bolster productivity among workers, and permitted—even encouraged—small private business ventures of all sorts. It was "better to be poor under socialism than rich under capitalism," Mao had preached during the Cultural Revolution.[6] In sharp contrast to the late chairman, Deng asserted that "poverty is not socialism" and "to get rich is glorious."[7]

Deng's market-oriented reforms were stunningly successful. By the mid-1990s, China was in the midst of an unprecedented economic boom that had brought a significantly higher standard of living for much of its vast population. Under Deng's equally market-oriented successors, Jiang Zemin and Hu Jintao, China's economy has continued to flourish, with its gross national product (GNP) growing at an impressive average annual rate of nearly 10 percent during the past two decades. (The GNP is the total value of goods and services a nation produces within a given time frame.) During the same period, the per capita disposable income of urban and rural households rose by nearly 300 and 400 percent, respectively. As of 2008, there were 120 million privately owned cars in China. In 1976, when the Cultural Revolution ended, there had not been a single one.

While China's top leaders in the post-Mao era have embraced economic reform, they have firmly rejected any

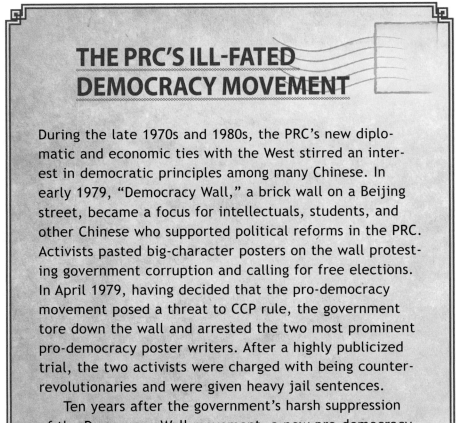

THE PRC'S ILL-FATED DEMOCRACY MOVEMENT

During the late 1970s and 1980s, the PRC's new diplomatic and economic ties with the West stirred an interest in democratic principles among many Chinese. In early 1979, "Democracy Wall," a brick wall on a Beijing street, became a focus for intellectuals, students, and other Chinese who supported political reforms in the PRC. Activists pasted big-character posters on the wall protesting government corruption and calling for free elections. In April 1979, having decided that the pro-democracy movement posed a threat to CCP rule, the government tore down the wall and arrested the two most prominent pro-democracy poster writers. After a highly publicized trial, the two activists were charged with being counter-revolutionaries and were given heavy jail sentences.

Ten years after the government's harsh suppression of the Democracy Wall movement, a new pro-democracy movement developed among students in Beijing who were meaningful political reform for the PRC. Although Chinese citizens enjoy considerably more freedom than they did during the Cultural Revolution, the government "continues to act aggressively to crack down on any signs of organized political opposition," observe authors Jiang and Ashley.[8] More than three decades after Mao's death, the PRC remains a one-party authoritarian state in which any perceived threats to CCP control are swiftly squelched, as demonstrated by the government's brutal repression of the student pro-democracy movement of 1989 and, more recently, by the arrest and imprisonment of

mourning the death of Hu Yaobang, a reform-minded CCP official. When thousands of students assembled in Tiananmen Square to honor Hu's memory in April 1989, the gathering quickly turned into a pro-democracy demonstration. Although at first the government's response was lenient, when the students fashioned a 33-foot (10-meter) papier-mâché "Goddess of Democracy" statue and erected it in the square on May 30, Deng's patience with the activists ran out. After the demonstrators refused to evacuate Tiananmen Square, PLA tanks and troops smashed the makeshift blockades around the square that had been erected by sympathetic Beijing residents and began firing on the unarmed protestors late on the night of June 3. The result was a massacre that left an estimated 1,500 protestors and local residents dead—although the government admitted to a death toll of only 300. More than 20 years after the Tiananmen massacre, the CCP still maintained that the demonstrations of May and June 1989 were counterrevolutionary acts and that Deng's harsh suppression of the pro-democracy movement was therefore completely justified.

the well-known Beijing dissident Hu Jia, for demanding democratic reforms.

THE CULTURAL REVOLUTION'S TOLL ON THE CHINESE PEOPLE

Aside from the enormous damage inflicted on the country's
cultural heritage by the Red Guards' wanton destruction of
ancient artwork, books, temples, and monuments, the Cultural Revolution's most obvious consequence for China was
the immense human suffering it caused. Scholars are unsure
how many people were killed or committed suicide as a
result of the brutal campaign, but most estimate the death
toll to be between 3 and 4 million. Millions more never fully
recovered from the physical or psychological abuse they were
subjected to, whether at Red Guard–led struggle sessions or in
government-run prisons and labor camps. Relatives, friends,
neighbors, and coworkers, whether motivated by genuine
"revolutionary zeal" or by fears for their own reputations or
lives, viciously turned on one another during the Cultural
Revolution, leaving "a bitter legacy of grief, distrust, hatred,
and a thirst for revenge," writes Maurice Meisner.[9] In many
cases, sons and daughters were estranged from their parents
when they, as adolescents or adult children of persecuted intellectuals and other "bad elements," sought to prove their own
revolutionary fervor by vandalizing their parents' homes or
physically assaulting them.

Among the Cultural Revolution's millions of victims was
virtually an entire generation of Chinese—the self-named "Lost
Generation," who already were attending or would shortly be
attending secondary school or college in 1966. For a substantial
portion of the Lost Generation, the Cultural Revolution was an
educational and professional disaster. During the chaotic early
stages of the movement, all universities and most secondary
schools were closed throughout the PRC. When the schools
gradually started to reopen in the late 1960s and early 1970s,

For many young Chinese, the Cultural Revolution is ancient history, but membership in the Communist Party is still seen as a way to advance in Chinese society. Here a young girl poses in 2008 beside a rusting Cultural Revolution statue depicting Red Guards chanting political slogans.

they did so with vastly watered-down curriculums (in keeping with the Cultural Revolution's emphasis on revolutionary purity over academic learning), robbing students of the chance to develop their intellectual and professional abilities. The majority of the estimated 12 million urban youth compelled to move to the countryside between 1969 and 1976 to "learn from the peasants" never earned a higher degree at all. Following his second rehabilitation by the CCP in 1977, Deng Xiaoping

THE CULTURAL REVOLUTION MUSEUM

Since the Central Committee published its official version of the Cultural Revolution's origins in 1981, the PRC's leadership has made every effort to discourage public discussion of the destructive movement. Nonetheless, in January 2005, in a remote, hilly area near the city of Shantou in Guangdong province, Peng Qian, the city's former deputy mayor, used private donations to found a museum devoted entirely to the revolution. Himself a former target of the Red Guards, the 74-year-old Peng was determined that his compatriots, including those born long after the Cultural Revolution ended in 1976, remember and learn from the mistakes of the most tumultuous era in the PRC's history.

Housed in a temple-like building, the museum's exhibits include dozens of photographs showing victims of the revolution—from well-known cultural and political figures to ordinary schoolteachers—being tormented at mass political meetings or paraded through the streets of their hometowns in tall dunce hats. Other photos depict children weeping over the bodies of dead parents, a bloodied angrily accused the Cultural Revolution's official scapegoats, the Gang of Four, of creating "an entire generation of mental cripples."[10] In the 1980s, determined to reverse the grave harm done to China's educational system and to help the PRC catch up to the rest of the developed world in the critical areas of science and technology, Deng initiated comprehensive reforms of the country's secondary school and college curriculums, teaching practices, and admission standards.

"rightist" being carted away in a basket after a brutal struggle session, and millions of young people at a Red Guard rally in Tiananmen Square ecstatically waving their Little Red Books of Mao's quotations.

Although the Chinese government has allowed the museum to remain open, Beijing clearly wants to call as little attention to it as possible. After several newspapers published favorable stories about Peng's project in early 2005, Beijing responded by prohibiting the Chinese media from writing about the museum in the future. This has not stopped thousands of people from visiting the museum, however, which is especially popular among the "Lost Generation" of Chinese, who were teenagers or young adults during the Cultural Revolution. One such visitor, who described himself as "a former Beijing Red Guard," expressed his gratitude to Peng for founding the museum in a poignant note in the guests' log. "The Chinese people," he wrote, "should take responsibility for their history, not only remember the glorious achievements, but also examine the shame."*

* Quoted in Edward Cody, "Chinese Museum Looks Back in Candor: Groundbreaking New Exhibit on Cultural Revolution Sparks Official Displeasure but Visitors' Praise." *Washington Post*, June 3, 2005, p. A17.

THE CULTURAL REVOLUTION AND CHINA'S RISE TO WORLD POWER

Many scholars have argued that while the Cultural Revolution caused tremendous human suffering, the movement also helped lay the groundwork for the very un-Maoist economic reforms of Deng Xiaoping. Because of the widespread havoc and chaos the Cultural Revolution created, these scholars argue, Deng did not have to contend with a powerful leftist backlash when he abandoned Mao's radical economic program in favor of market-oriented policies. In fact, the majority of the CCP's leadership and rank-and-file backed Deng's sweeping reforms. "A common verdict" among scholars of modern China, write MacFarquhar and Schoenhals, "is: no Cultural Revolution, no economic reform. The Cultural Revolution was so great a disaster that it provoked an even more profound cultural revolution, precisely the one that Mao intended to forestall." When Deng and the rest of the PRC's new moderate leadership successfully guided a willing China down the "capitalist road" during the last two decades of the twentieth century, the two authors contend, "Mao's worst revisionist nightmare had been realized, with only himself to blame."[11]

Over the past three decades, the Chinese economy's rapid expansion has transformed the PRC into an economic powerhouse. Some economists predict that the PRC, which currently has the largest population of any country in the world at 1.3 billion, also will have the globe's largest economy by 2050. The PRC is now believed to be the world's second-biggest military spender after the United States and is quickly becoming one of the world's greatest polluters because of China's heavy reliance on coal to spur its rapid industrial growth.

Worried about the movement's effect on the CCP's reputation, China's Communist leadership has sought to suppress public discussion of the traumatic decade ever since the Central Committee released its official verdict on the Cultural Revolution's origins in 1981. Xu Youyu, a political philosophy professor at the Chinese

Pictured, the skyline of modern Shanghai. In the twenty-first century, China is a global economic superpower. For many, living standards have improved dramatically in recent decades, although political controls remain tight.

Academy of Social Sciences and a former Red Guard, is one of the few Chinese who has dared to speak out against the regime's efforts to make the Cultural Revolution a taboo subject. Recently Xu, who is writing a history of the movement, remarked to an American journalist: "Those 10 years are a historical vacuum. The government has tried to erase them." Yet, he contends, it is critical that his fellow citizens study the fanatic violence and senseless waste of that pivotal decade: "Today few people think about the Cultural Revolution," he observes, "but we must know our history to learn from it."[12] Only then, Xu argues, can China ensure that the painful mistakes of the Cultural Revolution will never be repeated.

CHRONOLOGY

1921   Mao Zedong helps create the Chinese Communist Party (CCP).

1935   Mao becomes the unofficial leader of the CCP at the Zunyi Conference.

1949   The People's Republic of China (PRC) proclaimed by Mao.

1958   Mao launches his disastrous Great Leap Forward economic program.

1959   Mao replaces Defense Minister Peng Dehuai with Lin Biao.

TIMELINE

1965
Wu Han's play *The Dismissal of Hai Rui From Office* attacked on Mao's orders.

1949
People's Republic of China proclaimed by Mao.

1921

1966

1921
Mao Zedong helps create the Chinese Communist Party (CCP).

1966
Radical protests on Chinese campuses erupt; first Red Guard units formed; CCP Central Committee formally launches Cultural Revolution in August; Liu Shaoqi demoted; Lin Biao declared number two CCP leader.

1965   Wu Han's play *The Dismissal of Hai Rui From Office* attacked on Mao's orders; Luo Ruiqing, PLA chief of staff, is purged.

1966   Radical protests on Chinese campuses erupt; first Red Guard units formed; CCP Central Committee formally launches Cultural Revolution; Liu Shaoqi demoted; Lin Biao declared number two CCP leader.

1967   Violence between various radical groups becomes widespread; Mao calls on the PLA to restore order as fighting continues.

1968   Mao officially demobilizes the Red Guards in response to ongoing violence; urban students sent to the countryside to "learn from the peasants."

1968
Mao officially demobilizes the Red Guards in response to ongoing violence.

1971
Lin Biao dies mysteriously after allegedly trying to overthrow Mao.

1967   1976

1967
Violence between various radical groups becomes widespread; Mao calls on the PLA to restore order in September as fighting continues.

1976
Mao dies in September; Cultural Revolution ends in October with arrest of radical "Gang of Four."

1969   Mao officially designates Lin Biao as his successor; Liu Shaoqi dies in prison.

1971   Lin Biao dies mysteriously after allegedly trying to overthrow Mao.

1972   Historic meeting between Mao and President Richard Nixon in Beijing.

1976   Popular demonstrations in memory of Premier Zhou Enlai suppressed; Mao dies; Cultural Revolution ends with arrest of radical Gang of Four.

1980   Moderate Deng Xiaoping becomes the PRC's supreme leader.

NOTES

CHAPTER 1

1. Quoted in Michael Schoenhals, ed., *China's Cultural Revolution, 1966–1969: Not a Dinner Party.* Armonk, N.Y.: M.E. Sharpe, 1996, p. 106.

2. Quoted in Schoenhals, ed., *China's Cultural Revolution*, p. 33.

3. Quoted in Schoenhals, ed., *China's Cultural Revolution*, p. 47.

CHAPTER 2

1. Philip Short, *Mao: A Life.* New York: Macmillan, 2001, p. 21.

2. Jung Chang and Jon Halliday, *Mao: The Unknown Story.* New York: Alfred A. Knopf, 2005, p. 8.

3. Quoted in Short, *Mao: A Life*, p. 84.

4. Quoted in Jonathan Spence, *Mao Zedong.* New York: Penguin Books, 1999, p. 75.

5. Spence, *Mao Zedong*, p. 97.

6. Quoted in Short, *Mao: A Life*, p. 387.

7. Ibid.

8. Chang and Halliday, *Mao: The Unknown Story*, p. 278.

9. Quoted in Short, *Mao: A Life*, p. 392.

10. Quoted in Spence, *Mao Zedong*, p. 101.

CHAPTER 3

1. Quoted in Short, *Mao: A Life*, p. 419.

2. Quoted in Chang and Halliday, *Mao: The Unknown Story*, p. 426.

3. Quoted in Stanley Karnow, *Mao and China: A Legacy of Turmoil*, rev. ed. New York: Penguin Books, 1990, p. 88.

4. Lawrence R. Sullivan, *Historical Dictionary of the People's Republic of China.* Lanham, Md.: Scarecrow Press, 2007, p. 29.

5. Quoted in Shaun Breslin, *Mao.* New York: Longman, 1998, p. 98.

6. Spence, *Mao Zedong*, p. 146.

7. Quoted in Karnow, *Mao and China*, pp. 126–127.

8. Quoted in Maurice Meisner, *Mao's China and After: A History of the People's Republic*, 3rd ed. New York: Simon & Schuster, 1999, p. 293.

9. Quoted in Short, *Mao: A Life*, p. 523.

10. Quoted in Roderick MacFarquhar and Michael Schoenhals, *Mao's Last Revolution.* Cambridge, Mass.: Harvard University Press, 2006, p. 13.

11. Quoted in Short, *Mao: A Life*, pp. 525–526.

CHAPTER 4

1. Quoted in Short, *Mao: A Life*, pp. 525–526.

2. Quoted in Short, *Mao: A Life*, p. 531.

3. Quoted in Meisner, *Mao's China*, p. 313.

4. Quoted in Short, *Mao: A Life*, p. 528.

5. MacFarquhar and Schoenhals, *Mao's Last Revolution*, p. 28.

6. Quoted in MacFarquhar and Schoenhals, *Mao's Last Revolution*, p. 30.

7. Quoted in Schoenhals, ed., *China's Cultural Revolution*, p. 362.

8. Quoted in Short, *Mao: A Life*, p. 534.

9. Quoted in MacFarquhar and Schoenhals, *Mao's Last Revolution*, p. 27.

10. Quoted in J.A.G. Roberts, *Modern China: An Illustrated History*. Gloucestershire, U.K.: Sutton Publishing, 1998, p. 251.

11. Quoted in Short, *Mao: A Life*, p. 536.

12. Ibid.

13. Sullivan, *Historical Dictionary of the People's Republic of China*, p. 483.

14. MacFarquhar and Schoenhals, *Mao's Last Revolution*, pp. 63–64.

15. Quoted in Short, *Mao: A Life*, p. 538.

16. Quoted in Schoenhals, ed., *China's Cultural Revolution*, p. 363.

17. Quoted in Spence, *Mao Zedong*, p. 157.

18. Quoted in Short, *Mao: A Life*, p. 539.

19. Quoted in Short, *Mao: A Life*, p. 540.

20. Quoted in MacFarquhar and Schoenhals, *Mao's Last Revolution*, p. 90.

21. Quoted in MacFarquhar and Schoenhals, *Mao's Last Revolution*, pp. 92–93.

22. Short, *Mao: A Life*, p. 541.

CHAPTER 5

1. Quoted in Meisner, *Mao's China and After*, p. 318.

2. Quoted in MacFarquhar and Schoenhals, *Mao's Last Revolution*, p. 92.

3. Quoted in Short, *Mao: A Life*, p. 547 and Schoenhals, ed., *China's Cultural Revolution*, p. 4.

4. Short, *Mao: A Life*, p. 543.

5. Quoted in MacFarquhar and Schoenhals, *Mao's Last Revolution*, p. 111.

6. Quoted in Schoenhals, ed., *China's Cultural Revolution*, p. 33.

7. Quoted in Schoenhals, ed., *China's Cultural Revolution*, p. 200.

8. Schoenhals, ed., *China's Cultural Revolution*, p. 145.

9. Meisner, *Mao's China and After*, p. 315.

10. Quoted in Dahpon David Ho, "To Protect and Preserve: Resisting the Destroy the Four Olds Campaign, 1966–1967," in Joseph W. Esherick, Paul G. Pickowicz, and Andrew G. Walder, eds., *The Chinese Cultural Revolution as History*. Stanford, Calif.: Stanford University Press, 2006, p. 64.

11. Ho, "To Protect and Preserve," p. 78.

12. Yarong Jiang and David Ashley, *Mao's Children in the New China: Voices From the Red*

Guard Generation. New York: Routledge, 2000, p. 5.

13. Gao Yuan, *Born Red: A Chronicle of the Cultural Revolution.* Stanford, Calif.: Stanford University Press, 1987, p. 86.

14. MacFarquhar and Schoenhals, *Mao's Last Revolution,* p. 102.

15. Quoted in Schoenhals, ed., *China's Cultural Revolution,* p. 3.

CHAPTER 6

1. Quoted in Schoenhals, ed., *China's Cultural Revolution,* p. 365.

2. Quoted in Short, *Mao: A Life,* p. 557.

3. Quoted in Schoenhals, ed., *China's Cultural Revolution,* pp. 59–60.

4. Quoted in Roberts, *Modern China,* p. 254.

5. Meisner, *Mao's China and After,* p. 334.

6. Quoted in Meisner, *Mao's China and After,* pp. 336, 338.

7. Quoted in MacFarquhar and Schoenhals, *Mao's Last Revolution,* p. 221.

8. Quoted in Meisner, *Mao's China and After,* p. 340.

9. Quoted in Roberts, *Modern China,* p. 254.

10. Quoted in Meisner, *Mao's China and After,* p. 341.

11. Short, *Mao: A Life,* p. 568.

12. Quoted in Short, *Mao: A Life,* p. 573.

13. Jiang and Ashley, *Mao's Children in the New China,* p. 6.

14. Quoted in Schoenhals, ed., *China's Cultural Revolution,* p. 378.

15. Quoted in Schoenhals, ed., *China's Cultural Revolution,* p. 370.

16. Quoted in MacFarquhar and Schoenhals, *Mao's Last Revolution,* p. 279.

17. Quoted in Schoenhals, ed., *China's Cultural Revolution,* pp. 371, 31.

CHAPTER 7

1. Quoted in Meisner, *Mao's China and After,* p. 348.

2. Quoted in Margaret MacMillan, *Nixon and Mao: The Week That Changed the World.* New York: Random House, 2007, p. 205.

3. Quoted in Patricia Buckley Ebrey, *The Cambridge Illustrated History: China.* Cambridge, U.K.: Cambridge University Press, 1996, p. 319.

4. MacFarquhar and Schoenhals, *Mao's Last Revolution,* p. 341.

5. Quoted in MacFarquhar and Schoenhals, *Mao's Last Revolution,* p. 381.

6. Quoted in Short, *Mao: A Life,* p. 610.

7. Quoted in Short, *Mao: A Life,* p. 623.

8. Spence, *Mao Zedong,* p. 177.

CHAPTER 8

1. MacFarquhar and Schoenhals, *Mao's Last Revolution,* p. 456.

2. Quoted in Schoenhals, ed., *China's Cultural Revolution,* pp. 296–297.

3. MacFarquhar and Schoenhals, *Mao's Last Revolution,* p. 457.

4. MacFarquhar and Schoenhals, *Mao's Last Revolution,* p. 2.

5. Quoted in MacFarquhar and Schoenhals, *Mao's Last Revolution*, p. 148.

6. Quoted in Ebrey, *The Cambridge Illustrated History: China*, p. 322.

7. Quoted in MacMillan, *Nixon and Mao*, p. 331.

8. Jiang and Ashley, *Mao's Children in the New China*, p. 8.

9. Meisner, *Mao's China and After*, p. 355.

10. Quoted in Ebrey, *The Cambridge Illustrated History: China*, p. 323.

11. MacFarquhar and Schoenhals, *Mao's Last Revolution*, pp. 3, 459.

12. Quoted in Craig Simons, "Cultural Revolution Haunts China: It's Taboo to Speak of the Crimes of the Regime's Founder, but Some Want Truth Aired," *Atlanta Journal Constitution*, September 17, 2006, p. A4.

BIBLIOGRAPHY

Breslin, Shaun. *Mao*. New York: Longman, 1998.

Chang, Jung, and Jon Halliday. *Mao: The Unknown Story*. New York: Alfred A. Knopf, 2005.

Cody, Edward. "Chinese Museum Looks Back in Candor: Groundbreaking New Exhibit on Cultural Revolution Sparks Official Displeasure but Visitors' Praise." *Washington Post*, June 3, 2005.

Ebrey, Patricia Buckley. *The Cambridge Illustrated History: China*. Cambridge, U.K.: Cambridge University Press, 1996.

Esherick, Joseph W., Paul G. Pickowicz, and Andrew G. Walder, eds. *The Chinese Cultural Revolution as History*. Stanford, Calif.: Stanford University Press, 2006.

Jiang, Yarong, and David Ashley. *Mao's Children in the New China: Voices From the Red Guard Generation*. New York: Routledge, 2000.

Karnow, Stanley. *Mao and China: A Legacy of Turmoil*. Rev. ed. New York: Penguin Books, 1990.

MacFarquhar, Roderick, and Michael Schoenhals. *Mao's Last Revolution*. Cambridge, Mass.: Harvard University Press, 2006.

MacMillan, Margaret. *Nixon and Mao: The Week That Changed the World*. New York: Random House, 2007.

Meisner, Maurice. *Mao's China and After: A History of the People's Republic*. 3rd ed. New York: Simon & Schuster, 1999.

Roberts, J.A.G. *Modern China: An Illustrated History*. Gloucestershire, U.K.: Sutton Publishing, 1998.

Schoenhals, Michael, ed. *China's Cultural Revolution, 1966–1969: Not a Dinner Party*. Armonk, N.Y.: M.E. Sharpe, 1996.

Short, Philip. *Mao: A Life*. New York: Macmillan, 2001.

Simons, Craig. "Cultural Revolution Haunts China: It's Taboo to Speak of the Crimes of the Regime's Founder, but Some Want Truth Aired." *Atlanta Journal Constitution*, September 17, 2006.

Spence, Jonathan. *Mao Zedong*. New York: Penguin Books, 1999.

Sullivan, Lawrence R. *Historical Dictionary of the People's Republic of China*. Lanham, Md.: Scarecrow Press, 2007.

Yuan, Gao. *Born Red: A Chronicle of the Cultural Revolution*. Stanford, Calif.: Stanford University Press, 1987.

FURTHER RESOURCES

BOOKS

Chen, Da. *China's Son: Growing Up in the Cultural Revolution.* New York: Delacorte Press, 2001.

Marrin, Albert. *Mao Tse-tung and His China.* New York: Viking, 1989.

Pietrusza, David. *The Chinese Cultural Revolution.* San Diego, Calif.: Lucent, 1997.

Slavicek, Louise Chipley. *Mao Zedong.* Philadelphia: Chelsea House, 2003.

Zhang, Ange. *Red Land Yellow River: A Story from the Cultural Revolution.* Toronto: Groundwood Books, 2004.

WEB SITES

China Today
  http:// www.chinatoday.com

Chinese Holocaust Memorial: We Will Never Forget You
  http://humanities.uchicago.edu/faculty/ywang/history/e_
  index.htm

Internet History Sourcebooks Project:
  China Since World War II: The Cultural Revolution
  http://www.fordham.edu/halsall/eastasia/eastasiasbook.
  html#China%20Since%20World%20War%20II

Mao Zedong (1893–1976): Asia Source Biography
  http://www.asiasource.org/society/mao.cfm

Mao Zedong Internet Archive
   http://www.marxists.org/reference/archive/mao/

Modern China: Washington State University Civilizations
   **http://www.wsu.edu:8001/~dee/MODCHINA/MOD
   CHINA.HTM**

PICTURE CREDITS

INDEX

ABOUT THE AUTHOR

LOUISE CHIPLEY SLAVICEK received her master's degree in history from the University of Connecticut. She is the author of numerous articles on American and world history for scholarly journals and young people's magazines, including *Cobblestone*, *Calliope*, and *Highlights for Children*. Her numerous books for young people include *Women of the American Revolution*, *Israel*, *Mao Zedong*, *The Great Wall of China*, and *Daniel Inouye*.